Only God Rescued Me

~*~

My Journey from
Satanic Ritual Abuse

~*~

Lisa Meister

There is a Line Publishing

Indianapolis, Indiana

Published by There is a Line Publishing
Indianapolis, Indiana
www.thereisalinepublishing.com

Printed in the United States of America

Lisa Meister has a passion for God, her family, and teaching, all in that order. She has homeschooled for the past nineteen years and prides herself in the fact that each of her brilliant children has been the valedictorian of his or her class. Lisa, her husband James, and their children are all active in their local church. You can find Lisa's blog at onlygodrescuedme.com. If you would like to contact Lisa for questions or speaking engagements, please email her at lisameister@onlygodrescuedme.com.

Names and places have been changed throughout this book to protect the innocent.

To my Heavenly Father ~
As the deer pants for the water, so my soul longs after you.

To my James ~
You were not only with me on the journey, but in every step. I would not have made it without you. Thank you, my precious love, and best friend.

Contents

Foreword

What if the Boko Haram was not in a third world country, but right here in the United States? This type of group is a criminal enterprise using a religious "shell" for the practice of trafficking women and children. Some members are "true believers" and some members are just sociopaths. What if Stranger Danger wasn't that unshaven man in the dark doorway, but was George, that nice man from church who volunteered alongside you at the fundraiser? Secretly, George is running a child porn ring, abusing his own children, and utilizing sophisticated conditioning and methods of torture to keep the children too afraid to run. Yet his smile is so lovely and he donates to good causes.

This is too horrible to imagine, so we won't think of it. To think of it would horrify us and we couldn't enjoy our football game, couldn't taste the sweetness of our latte, couldn't sleep at night. Let's call that crazy and move on. Unfortunately, we *dissociate* horrors. We make it disappear, so we can function. We do this consciously, and in a multitude of ways; we do it without even thinking. We resist noticing, in order to manage our lives. We can take it in small doses, like the face of the shocked child in the bombing. We send $100 to the Red Cross, mention it on Facebook, and then try to forget.

We are good at forgetting. It's the mind's way of protecting itself. While some bad memories never seem to leave us, horrible trauma can be blocked from awareness because our brain says, "Oh G-d no, this cannot be true and I still live." It can be blocked automatically, without conscious thought, but it leaves a little "rough spot," where in its place there is a distracted stare, a nervous habit, a bad dream perhaps. For some reason, a person then finds it harder to function, to get laundry done, to leave the house, but has no idea why it seems to take so much energy to get through the day. The brain is working so hard to keep that memory away, that normal functioning becomes less efficient.

Some survivors of severe and repeated trauma dissociate so early in life and to such a degree, that their very sense of self is "in pieces." After all, this horrible stuff could not have happened to *me*. I can float out of my body and then it happened to *her*. This is the mechanism, in the briefest of terms, of Dissociative Identity Disorder (DID).

People like Lisa Meister have come to me, at first not sure why their life "isn't working." They suspect something happened, and are getting flashbacks in pieces. Over time, their mind begins to release the story to their conscious awareness, and the horror returns. This is not something that anyone would want to experience. Who would want this to be true? These people do not volunteer for this, they do not want attention, and they are frightened of what memories come next. Freddy Krueger has nothing on this. Recovery from these abuses is a very, very challenging experience.

Courage is being afraid and doing it anyway. Lisa Meister has done this. *She tells.* She tells her story, from at first only recalling an ideal childhood, to the dawning of her memories. She tells of the havoc this knowing has brought to her life, of the backlash from family members, and the physical problems she suffers which are highly correlated with the experience of severe trauma. She also tells of the loving support of her husband and her faith. Despite Lisa's experience of a twisted form of faith-based abuse, she never allowed it to diminish her spiritual relationship with The Divine. This mainstay remained intact, providing her guidance and comfort. In this memoir, Lisa chronicles her life and recovery thus far. Truly, she has been to Hell and back, and refuses to be silent. She will continue to tell, and by telling she will help many.

Once she had told, and we know, it is then our responsibility to hold it in our awareness, and to advocate for prevention, intervention and treatment.

Bravo, Lisa.

Willa Wertheimer, Psy.D.
Clinical Psychologist
Director, Fellow, The International Society for the Study of Trauma and Dissociation (ISSTD)

Introduction

I watched her as she came into the store. I was behind the counter and she never looked up. Never. She was near perfect with her blond hair neatly combed, a small barrette, and every hair in place. Her white cardigan sweater and Bobby-Brooks styled dress accented her perfection. When she did glance at me, it was only in response to my "Hello, Lisa." Her smile was soft and her reply had been properly rehearsed.

I heard her dad snap a question at her and watched as her head jerked sideways. Instantly, she paid attention to what he was saying... yet I never put two and two together. After all, he often snapped at his employees and was very demanding; it was his nature. He was a task master and in control of his surroundings at all times. He was also inappropriate with his comments and touches toward me, but I needed the job and had learned to tolerate his behavior.

He boasted of his children's skills, they were at the top of their class. I remember him expecting nothing less than excellence. 'What was his issue,' I thought? It wasn't my business, or was it? How was I to know that the little girl standing in front of me was a victim of Satanic Ritual Abuse? She had no outward markings and although I had heard rumors that Satanic Covens were prominent in our county, I never pieced the stories together ~ not until a mentally ill, foster daughter came to live with me. Her tales were of law enforcement taking her for rides in their cars and delivering her to remote areas. Satanic images, sexual abuse, pregnancy, drugs, and the diagnosis of "schizophrenic" had followed her throughout the court system. She was told not to speak of it; it was all her imagination, and I was to pacify her nightmares – which wasn't hard to do given the amount of mind numbing drugs she had been prescribed.

My husband and I shared pizza one evening with Lisa and her family. Everyone knows that pizza is normally eaten on paper plates with laughter, soda, and silliness. When I alluded to this, I was politely told that paper plates were not allowed in the house. I chuckled aloud, thinking it to be a joke. It was not.

Not a child cracked a smile at the table or talked out of place. It was all too obvious that every detail was being controlled and with just a look you understood that 'elbows were to be off the table and napkins were to be used.' The conversation was strained and formal, with "yes, please" and "no, thank you" and I thought, 'these are the most well-behaved children I have ever seen.' The evening was awkwardly painful and my husband and I left confused at what we were seeing. "Wow," I said. "That was weird. It was as if they had rehearsed the whole evening ahead of time. I'd hate to live in that family."

In writing this, I recall the little girl who refused to look up, staring at her feet, and I finally understand. A prominent businessman, a town doctor, law enforcement and state officials: I knew them all personally. I worked with them. I heard the rumors and rumblings, but the conspiracy theories were extreme, and the investigations had always run up against brick walls. "We were the smallest county in the state, yet boasted the most children taken from their homes.

Rumor had it that "the children were being sold for adoption," or was it for something else?

~Catherine

Psalm 142: 4-6

Look and see, there is no one at my right hand; no one is concerned for me, and I have no refuge; no one cares for my life. I cry to you, Lord; I say, "You are my refuge, my portion in the land of the living." Listen to my cry, for I am in desperate need; rescue me from those who pursue me, for they are too strong for me. (KJV)

My Life

~*~

How can I tell you how my life has been
When the telling of it is so very grim
That I don't even want to think through it again

How can I get you to see through my eyes
How little I was, so tiny in size
When terror before me…materialized

How can you feel the emotions raw
Roiling and boiling inside my craw
If I am unable to tell you it all

How can you hear all the tale I tell
If it were complete your dreams would be hell
Terror grabbing you under its spell

Can I tell you enough for you to see
What has happened to so many like me
To open your eyes as gently can be

I will give it my best, I shall try to be wise
To give you perspective, to see with fresh eyes
What the devil meant for harm, God turned into a prize

There is one more thing I'd like to say
Before you turn page and go on your way
Please for all us survivors
Pray

Shattering the Fairytale

~*~

I could feel my husband's eyes on me as I knelt on my hands and knees, giving the kitchen linoleum the cleaning of its life. James cautiously watched for a little while and then asked, "Lisa, what's the matter?"

"He's buddying up to her. He's buddying up to our Stephanie!"

At this point, my attack on the linoleum was becoming manic. The Pine Sol was burning my hands as the friction of the rag scoured the same spot over and over on the floor. The confusion in the room was tangible as James tried to grasp what I was saying.

My parents had been at our house that afternoon. Father had set a tent up in the living room for our five-year-old daughter Stephanie. He was playing with her while at the same time, deliberately causing our three-year-old son, Daniel, to cry by refusing him access into the tent. Later at dinner while we were all eating cake, Stephanie began scooping the icing off her piece and eating it. James told her to eat the cake and not just the icing. Immediately, Father scooped a big spoonful of icing off his cake and put it in Stephanie's mouth, challenging James with an arrogant stare.

"Who's buddying up to Stephanie?" James tried again.

"Father is! He's buddying up to her! You can't let him. You can't let him!" I was hysterical and sounded irrational.

21

"Okaaaay, what would he do to her?"

At this point I slumped my shoulders. "I don't know. I don't know. But you can't let him!" And with this, I burst into tears.

Once upon a time in a land far away, a little girl was born into a large and loving family. Her cradle was rocked by grandparents, many aunts and uncles, and bunches of cousins whom she grew to love. But just as the world around her began to take form, Father moved their family to a small town in Minnesota, where she would live the next sixteen years of her life in a make-believe castle.

The paradise of Minnesota was a child's playground. Many feet of snow fell each year and covered the ground in winter's white. She learned to make snow angels and snowmen, and loved to go sledding with her brothers. In the summer, she formed sandcastles, roamed beaches, traipsed woodland trails, and enjoyed family picnics. As autumn leaves turned bronze and gold, she thought there was nothing lovelier than her perfect world.

Her parents were traditional. Father went to work every day and Mother was a housewife. Every year they would return to the grandparent's family farm and visit with each of the aunts, uncles, and cousins. Having such a family was as jewels in her crown. Those were the times that brought her the greatest joy. They were her favorite memories.

She and her three brothers reminisced of those moments back on the farm and often the young girl would daydream of the day when she would be able to live near her family again in Wisconsin. Having family brought her such joy that she never wanted to leave them and go back to the small town in Minnesota. But every year when their vacation was over, Father would load the car and reluctantly they would return to her imaginary kingdom.

The young princess reveled in amazement that she was so loved and cared for. She would watch other children whose families were not half as grand as hers, and she felt sorry for those who did not live within her fairytale. Father, Mother, and the little girl's three brothers had created a life near-perfect.

When she was seven, her parents began to attend a little country church in town where the young girl heard of Jesus and His love for her. Pastor Molnar loved God with all his heart and was the kindest shepherd she had ever known. Because of him, she learned to love God also. One day, her parents left the little country church to return to their traditional place of worship. How she missed Pastor Molnar and his message of hope. Jesus had become her best friend.

From a teenage perspective, the young woman's life was perfection. She excelled in sports and academics, graduating valedictorian of her class. As senior class president, she had numerous honors, trophies, medals and scholarships, and was accepted to The University of Minnesota. There, she met her future husband, James, at a Christian group on campus. They were married soon after she graduated. With her bachelor's degree in education, she landed a teaching job in the inner city of Chicago where she taught while her husband finished his PhD.

Within a few years, the young woman got busy having children, and retired from public teaching to stay at home and raise her own babies. Like clockwork, a new baby arrived every two years. With three children in four years, diaper duty and laundry was never ending.

James' parents graciously gave the couple an acre of land on which to build their first home, and their own fairytale began to take shape. The young woman was able to pick out a beautiful house from an architectural magazine and design the interior floor plan herself. Her castle had every luxury a little girl could imagine and was filled with such love. Her life was a dream come true.

The rhythm of day to day living began to take on its own magic as the young woman homeschooled their children, kept up with housework, church services, social activities, and extended family. "Happily ever after" would have happened had she not decided to invite Mother and Father over to dinner "that afternoon," for soon after, the fairytale life shattered into a thousand pieces and a nightmare began to emerge from the dark forest of her memories.

John 8:32

And ye shall know the truth,
and the truth shall make you free.
(KJV)

Song

"Household of Faith"
Steve Green (Household of Faith, 2015)

First Flashback

~*~

James and I moved into our new dream home. We had been moving every year or two our entire marriage, so finally putting down roots was a relief, and a big answer to prayer. While unpacking boxes, lost items showed up that were never opened in all the moves.

I opened a box labeled "Bedroom" and James smiled as I squealed with delight at my long lost, and much loved, Raggedy Ann doll. Her tattered body attested to her going everywhere with me for years. I grabbed Raggedy Ann from the box and squeezed her to my heart just as I had as a child. Suddenly, a burning ball of emotions exploded in my chest. I compare it to people who say their whole life flashed before their eyes before they died. Yet, I had no memories, just the unexpressed emotions of them.

I immediately yelped and threw Raggedy Ann down as if she had burned me. James and I stared in shock at my beloved doll sprawled on the floor. Like in a comedy, we both slowly raised our heads and looked at each other. "What was that?" James asked.

"I don't know," I whispered. I shrugged and tried my best to explain the feelings.

"If Raggedy Ann could talk, what would she tell you?" he asked.

"I have no idea."

I kept looking at my Raggedy Ann and was afraid of what would happen if I spent more time with her. My heart beat fast and

I was reeling from the intensity of the feelings that had just surfaced. I knew that I never wanted to feel them again. I was afraid to touch the doll, so James carefully picked her up and took the doll and box back to the attic. Whatever she had to say, I was not willing to hear.

The nightmares began the evening of the infamous dinner. Night after night, I would dream of getting raped by groups of men, never just one. The harder I tried to get away from the men, the more powerless I became. By day, I was confused and hurting – by night, I dreaded falling asleep. Once they started, they wouldn't stop. I would have nightmares nightly for years to come. I somehow knew that my body was trying to tell me something that my mind could not yet comprehend.

Prior to the start of the nightmares, I had experienced times of intense, emotional pain in the center of my chest. It was so strong that I could not stand it. There are no words to explain the extreme need to escape from the feeling of terror. The pressure of emotions would fill my chest and attempt to spill out. I forced myself to push the feelings back down, knowing that I was not going to try to figure them out. The only way I could deal with what was happening, was to stay hyper–busy and keep music going at all times. If I could do these things, I could pacify the intense pain.

A couple weeks after the dinner, I was lying in bed waiting for James to join me. All of a sudden, I could feel the sensation of a man's genitals being rubbed all over my face. I shrieked and kept rubbing my face, trying to get rid of the feeling. James ran to me, trying to figure out what just happened. He sat on the chair and pulled me onto his lap, holding me until the tears subsided.

"What is going on?" I cried, still rubbing my face.

James's voice was sad. "Lisa, I think you just had a bad memory."

We looked at each other and information started dropping into my head. It was 'a knowing,' though I had nothing to confirm that it was true.

"I would never accuse anyone of something I wasn't absolutely sure of, James. But everything inside me is saying it was Father, and Mother knew."

My mind fought valiantly to purge the idea, yet deep down I knew that it was true. The next time a memory hit, it was more graphic, but I still did not see the face of the perpetrator. After many weeks of this, the face finally emerged…it was Father.

With this realization, I cried and cried as I considered my options. I could say nothing and just pretend none of this happened or I could tell James what I was seeing. I knew how he would react. He would be repulsed by me and wouldn't want to be close with me anymore.

We had promised each other before we married that divorce would never be an option, so I knew he wouldn't leave me, but what if he just wanted to cohabitate? That thought terrified me. The only other option I knew was to allow this path of remembering and trust in God to lead the journey.

I pondered this for a very long time and prayed, asking God for guidance. Finally, I came to the realization that I did not really have a choice. If I didn't follow the truth, I would never be able to save my children from what happened to me. The courage of the mom rose up inside of me. I would do it for them.

~*~

Psalm 27:11

Teach me thy way, O Lord, and lead me in a plain path because of mine enemies. (KJV)

Joshua 1:9

Have not I commanded thee? Be strong and of a good courage; be not afraid, neither be thou dismayed: for the Lord thy God is with thee whithersoever thou goest. (KJV)

Song

"Beauty for Ashes"
Crystal Lewis (Lewis, 1996)

Starting To Get It

~*~

"Nancy, there's something wrong with me."

It was the summer before the infamous family dinner, and I had been sensing something changing in me.

"Like what?" she asked.

"Everything is falling apart around me and I can't keep up; I don't know why. I work all day long, yet at the end of the day it looks like I have accomplished nothing. It doesn't make any sense. Something inside keeps telling me that there's something really wrong, but I don't know what it is."

"Do you know what it is connected to?" she asked.

"I am deathly afraid of Father. James thinks it's because of not getting his approval. But I know that isn't it. I learned a long time ago that he never approved of anything I did."

"What are you afraid of then?" Nancy asked.

"I don't know." I shrugged my shoulders. "But whatever it is, it's really bad."

~*~

After the dinner, plagued with nightmares and flashbacks, I couldn't talk to my mother and not give away what was going on. She had been calling a lot and I had refused to answer the phone. When James did, I would tell him to give her an excuse that I couldn't talk right now. I was fragile and knew that all I would do was cry if I attempted to speak with her. Even if I wanted to share, I wouldn't know what to say or where to begin.

My mother knew something was wrong because I had never avoided her calls in the past. As weeks went on, I realized I was never going to feel strong enough to handle it, so I might as well get it over with. I finally accepted her call.

"Why haven't you wanted to talk to me?" she asked.

"I am dealing with some things I haven't dealt with before."

"Is it Father?"

"Yes," I slowly replied in disbelief. How did she know?

"It never happened," she instantly retorted.

"What never happened?"

She had no reply to this and quickly changed the subject. I could have been dealing with any number of issues concerning Father, so her statement shocked me. Why would she immediately go there? She refused to answer my question. If what was going on inside of me wasn't enough to figure out that I had been abused, her reaction certainly convinced me.

During another phone call, she asked, "Are you still having a hard time?"

"Yes."

"Just don't think about it," she advised. "Read Psalms and go on, otherwise, you won't be able to take care of your children."

"Think about what, Mother?" Again, she gave no reply and changed the subject.

These conversations had my mind whirling in circles that led to nowhere. She knew something and was talking to the part of me that knew what was going on, yet I was an outsider to the conversation. I had no idea what the conversations meant or what story they were telling.

Father had never been very nice to me. In front of others, he gave off the impression that he was just looking out for my welfare and I needed guidance; but in private, I knew him as cruel, emotionally abusive, and saw that he took pleasure in embarrassing me in front of others. I learned quickly as a child to conform and be on my best behavior – although, it never seemed to be enough to satisfy him.

Seeing him through the eyes of others was sobering to say the least. Those that worked closely with him in business, confirmed that the regimented control and drill–sergeant approach Father took toward me also carried into his professional life.

Proverbs 1: 5

A wise man will hear and will increase learning. (KJV)

Song

"Voice of Truth" Casting Crowns
(Steven Curtis Chapman, 2003)

survival by repression

i think amnesic thoughts
i cry silent tears
i die while I live
i open my mouth to a silent scream
i speak what i cannot say
i listen to what i cannot hear
i hear what is not being said
i see what isn't there
i tell what i do not know
i laugh so i will not cry
i run on legs that will not hold me
i protect myself with frozen arms
i go to bed for the horror i won't recall
i forget so i won't remember
i wake up and do it all over again
i survive because i am strong

Putting Pieces Together

I am four years old and in bed, clutching Raggedy Ann to my heart. My eyes are huge as Father sits on the edge of the bed, rubbing his hands between my legs.

"There, doesn't that feel good?" he croons in a sickly-sweet voice that he never used during the day.

It sort of did and sort of didn't, yet I didn't like it one bit. I was terrified, but there was no way that I was going to be able to tell him to stop. Pretty soon, I was just my eyes and didn't feel it anymore. (For more information on being "Just My Eyes", please see the explanation at the end of this chapter.)

~*~

In the midst of increasing flashbacks and nightmares, I realized I couldn't survive without answers. I went to the bookstore and grabbed the first self-help book on sexual abuse that I could find – The Wounded Heart: Hope for Adult Victims of Childhood Sexual Abuse, by Dr. Daniel Allender. I was so ashamed that I was a victim of abuse that I didn't want anyone to know and fled the store

That night, I started reading the book and was horrified at how closely it paralleled my life. "We grapple with the present, taking responsibility for current idolatry in the form of self-glorification and self-protection, then what is to be known about the past will be clear over time. In that sense, the past is the servant of the present and change in the present clears the way for whatever God wants us to know about the past." (Allender, 36)

God was using this process to tell me about my past, and if He was for figuring out my past, then I had to be also. This process was going to change me and I had to trust that God would make it for the better.

Dr. Allender explained how families were structured and behaved in order for sexual abuse to be allowed. It seemed to me that Allender was describing my family to a T. I was in shock. I kept wanting to find out that it was all a big mistake, but the more I learned, the more I saw that this was real and there was no going back.

I was reminded of my college years. My best friend, Nancy, came from an abusive home with an alcoholic father. I came from the home of the "perfect" Christian family. (I wholeheartedly believed that at the time.) Nancy and I would talk for hours about our families. What completely confused me was that our family dynamics were the same: hers with the abusive family and mine with the perfect one. It took years of those conversations with Nancy before I was able to look at my family and realize that maybe my childhood wasn't so perfect after all.

As I read the book, Dr. Allender talked about repression. "Repression is your mind creating a moment of amnesia in order to find a way to not think about abuse so that you can keep going on with your life." The more I read about it, the more I realized that Mother had taught me all of that. I learned repression from her:

"You're not remembering right."

"It would devastate Father if he knew that he had hurt you."

"You have to think of his reputation."

"Don't tell James or his family."

"This is just an attack from the enemy."

"Just listen to the Psalms, you'll feel better."

"Is your period due?"

"You're not telling anyone, are you? It's a family thing."

"I'm really uncomfortable with you talking with a counselor."

"I can't believe that you don't know Father loves you. He showed his love for you in so many ways."

"You can't think about this, Lisa. You need to take care of your family."

"It's not like you were ever abused."

"It didn't happen."

"You have your kids to take care of. You don't have time to think through things."

On and on it went during all of the phone calls she inundated me with. It was quite a revelation. The repercussions of this information were huge. I had already been wary of my mother and knew that I could not trust her any longer. Her continual comments only confirmed what I knew to be true: she was the one responsible for allowing the abuse to continue. I had been right. My mother knew and she was attempting to protect Father and her even now.

The sexual abuse by Father became a reality that I could no longer dismiss. I felt like someone had hit me with a hammer and had shattered me into a million pieces. I was left trying to put the pieces of this puzzle back together again. Often, I would pick up a piece and look at it closely to see if it was really who I was, or simply a reaction from the abuse. If it was from abuse I had to throw it out, but if it was really me, I had to put it back. I didn't realize it at the time (thank God), but this process was to take me the rest of my life.

As I stared at all the pieces, I understood why so many things never made sense. With the added knowledge of the abuse, my life was finally starting to fit together for the first time.

Some childhood memories were not repressed. I recall a time when I was about seven years old and told my mother that Father had hurt me. She defensively said, "No. He was just playing." (The only way he did "play" with my brothers and me, was by hurting us – in order to teach us how to deal with pain.) I repeated it again. "No. He hurt me down here…" and I pointed to my private area.

"No, Lisa," she corrected me, "he is just checking you for vaginal infections."

I reasoned with my childlike understanding, that "my reality was incorrect," so there was no point in expressing my pain. That was the last time I can remember trying to tell someone about what was happening. I never made sense of this memory, so I filed it in my "it doesn't make sense" box.

Another memory came to mind. Father showered with me, alone. His private area was at the same height as my eyes and although I was able to ignore it when I was little, I was repulsed by it when I got a few years older.

I never liked seeing Father naked. He would walk through the house naked my whole life. Not for long periods at any time, but to the bathroom, kitchen and back to his room. I finally told my mother how uncomfortable it made me feel to see him walking around naked and she informed me, "It was just a part of life." Apparently though, what I had shared was deemed important enough for her to confront Father and soon after, he began to wear underwear.

Looking back, this also didn't make much sense. I wondered why my mother did not take care of bathing me. Another one for 'The Box.'

I was very young when Father took me to visit a witch. This was strange for sure, but even stranger was the fact that he never took me anywhere by myself.

We stood at a door of a modular house. I was afraid of meeting her, but Father seemed calm. When the woman opened the door, I was surprised that she looked "normal." She didn't have a wart on her nose or a pointy black hat.

She eyed me over and then Father and she went into another room to talk. Looking back, there was no logic to this memory, so the visit with the witch was also put into the 'The Box.'

I pondered a memory from grade school: I was in sixth grade and waiting on the steps for the school bell to ring and the doors to open to allow us inside. Suddenly, someone pointed at me and told everyone that I had a hickey on my neck. Immediately, everyone started laughing and pointing. When the bell finally rang, I ran into the bathroom to look. Sure enough, there was a hickey on my neck. I spent days trying to figure out if there was any way that I could have given it to myself. (I had yet to have a boyfriend and was quite determined never to kiss.) The question lay unresolved in my mind, so I added it to the box of unanswered questions.

My parents always told me when I struggled with an emotional issue that it was because I was treated badly by kids at school. Now I realize that I had a pretty normal school life. I was treated the way many kids were. My concerns had nothing to do with grade school teasing or my quiet demeanor.

When James and I traveled home from college so that he could ask for my hand in marriage, everything had an eerie strangeness to it. I casually sat on the arm of Mother's chair and suggested going to the bedroom so James and Father could talk. Mother squeezed my arm tightly and hissed, "Don't do this to me!" Her reaction and response was so strange that I was taken aback by it.

Mother and I left Father and James alone for about half an hour to talk. No one came to tell us what happened, so we walked back into the living room to find out that permission had been granted, along with the promise that James and I would never put him (no mention of Mother) into a nursing home. That was his only stipulation.

Hearing the news, Mother whirled around and marched into the kitchen. She furiously scoured her pots and pans. She was intensely angry and I had never seen her like that. I swear she had steam coming out of her ears. Father's only comment was, "Well, I guess we're going to lose you."

The rest of the evening was tense and awkward. There were no congratulations, no hugs, no happiness and no talking about it at all. I felt like I was doing something terribly wrong.

The next morning, James and I went to my parents' church with them. When we arrived, Mother and Father had completely switched their behavior and became the excited parents, gushing about us getting married. It was the strangest thing to see them – like Jekyll and Hyde. After church, we felt the tension again. It made no sense. There were no objections or concerns about James at all, just the unexplained response. This only added to the growing pile of questions.

A newly married memory came to mind. James and I were laughing and play wrestling. He had me pinned on the floor, holding my wrists and I immediately started crying and shrieking. He jumped off of me quicker than I could have believed possible and helped me up. We just stared at each other – another one for "the box."

One day, early in our marriage, my parents and brothers were visiting James and me. While they were watching television, a sexy commercial came on. "It makes you want to do something with Stephanie, doesn't it?" Father said with a half-smile.

James was dumbfounded. He could not believe the comment made. "Only a sick person would even think like that!"

"Well, I think it's funny," my younger brother retorted.

James glared at my brother and snapped. "Well, I don't!"

He walked away and kept a close eye on our children from then on. This incident was added to our pile of unanswered questions. The strange behavior and comments were not adding up.

Another time we were spending the day at my parents' house. James and Father were talking in the formal living room. Father was telling James about a friend of his whose daughter had accused him (her father) of molesting her. Father claimed that this young girl had always been a liar and therefore the accusation was not true. He then shocked James by informing him that he himself had Mother call the doctor's office pretending to be me and had all my medical records sent to him so that I could "never accuse him of anything like that."

James was shocked and asked why Father would even think that I would make an accusation such as that. Immediately the subject changed.

We had Thanksgiving at Father and Mother's house, and it turned out to be the last one we would ever share with them. It was particularly puzzling. We had three children at the time, and I was about to take on a couple more for a while. A friend of mine had just given birth to twins and needed help, so I was going to watch the babies for a couple of weeks until she felt well enough to take their care back over.

My dear friend had been sexually abused by her step-dad and it had pushed her to the point of great illness. Since Mother had always wanted me to have twins, I thought she would enjoy talking with me about how to take care of them. I shared with my mother what my friend was going through and she immediately clammed up and refused to talk about the twins or help me plan for their care. My mother's behavior was really strange and it just didn't make any sense.

After dinner that night, Mother was sitting on the floor in front of the refrigerator trying to find space for all the Thanksgiving leftovers. I was leaning against the doorway, with James next to me and suddenly the words rolled out of me.

"You know, Mother, when James met me, he told me that my self-esteem was a little higher than a street person. He was right. You always told me that I had low self-esteem because of being treated badly by other students in school. But, I don't think that's it. I think I was treated like every other kid in school. It was something else."

Mother's head snapped up and her eyes bored into mine. "Have you told Father?"

The response was so abnormal that I scowled. "No...why?"

"Why not?" she said and she left it at that – discussion closed – another end to a crazy conversation. We were both communicating on some level, but I wasn't cognitively aware of what it was. It left me totally confused.

Two months later, we had the infamous dinner. That also didn't make sense at the time. With my decision to validate that I was indeed the survivor of sexual abuse from my Father, the pieces from my "this doesn't make sense" box started to fit together. They formed a strange puzzle of my life. Still, there were missing fragments that left me with unanswered questions. God was leading me to find the truth. He has a way of bringing truth to light. I concluded that this path was going to be very painful, but absolutely necessary.

Proverbs 3:5-6

Trust in the Lord with all thine heart; and lean not unto thine own understanding. In all thy ways acknowledge him, and he shall direct thy paths. (KJV)

Luke 8:17

For nothing is secret, that shall not be made manifest; (known) neither anything hid, that shall not be known and come abroad (exposed). (KJV)

Song

"Be Still"
Kari Jobe (Edward Cash, 2009)

"Just My Eyes"

~*~

God gives abuse victims ways to deal with the abuse. It doesn't take away the pain and suffering, but it does make the situation survivable. Survival comes very naturally to young children. Children can escape into their bodies, into an object that they see, or even the ceiling.

This phenomenon is called "dissociation." "It is a way to escape over-whelming stimulation or unpleasantness by creating a different reality." (Oksana, 2001, p. 56) I did this by having my body "disappear" until only my eyes were left. I would also escape into the left side of my brain and "hang out" there until the abuse was over. It doesn't mean there wasn't pain in my body, but it became bearable.

Sexually abused children can dissociate by focusing on an object and staring at it hard until that object is all there is. In SRA (Satanic Ritual Abuse), there were no safe objects to disappear into, so my brain was the constant that I needed.

A tremendous amount of attention is focused on manipulating dissociate in victims of ritual abuse. To achieve this, violators make use of human learning and developmental patterns. For example, it is known that most lifelong beliefs and resulting behaviors have their roots in the crucial early developmental years. It is also believed that dissociative learning happens more readily at this time. Therefore, cult indoctrination is likely concentrated before the age of six." (Oksana, 2001, p. 57)

I dissociated by going into my eyes. My body would just disappear and I would get the wonderful "I just really don't care what they are doing to me because I am not here" feeling. When the abuse was worse than 'usual,' I would disappear into the left side of my brain, tucked inside a place they could not access. I thank God for this ability. It enabled me to handle the pain and to compartmentalize so that I could get up in the morning as if nothing had happened and go to school with a sore and very tired body.

"Being just my eyes" and crawling into the left side of my brain was the best way I could escape. To this day, when I am becoming triggered, especially in counseling where we talk about specific elements of the abuse, I find myself just being my eyes.

The Talk

~*~

"You are thirteen now and I am going to teach you how to be a woman," Father said.

I always thought that if I pretended to be asleep Father would leave, but it never worked. Yet, I had no other strategy. This time, I had to start pleasing him instead of him taking advantage of me. It was so much worse and much more shame-filled.

Suddenly the door opened and in walked my mother. My mind instantly exhaled. 'Finally, someone saw what was happening and this nightmare would be over.' She stood in the doorway, and I could see her hands curled into fists; she kept clenching and unclenching.

"Get out of here!" he growled.

She paused a moment, turned, walked out and closed the door…

~*~

The flashbacks were horrible. I would be going about my normal daily routine when suddenly I would get extreme pain in a part of my body. The pain was real and would not go away; aspirin didn't touch it. The pain would stay for hours or days, and then my mind would flash the episode that perfectly explained the pain. It was awful and I was getting them one right after another. I was also still having the nightmares every night.

I was so ashamed that I was a sexual abuse survivor that I made James promise not to tell anyone. He finally reached his limit a couple weeks later and told me that he needed help and couldn't do it alone. I didn't blame him. He had three children under the age of five and a confused and constantly sobbing wife to take care of.

I agreed for him to share my experience with his mom. Sue was instantly at our house hugging me and telling me how sorry she was. Sue was a mom to me in ways Mother never could. She came often to help with the kids, to drop off a meal, to do my laundry, and to talk and pray with me. Whenever I needed her, she was there.

My next decision on my journey of truth was to get a counselor to help me through this craziness. I had never been to a counselor before, and no one had ever suggested I had been sexually abused before my first flashback. My first of many counselors was Janice, and she really helped me through the beginning stages of my recovery. She explained the importance of going to my parents and talking with them about what I knew about the sexual abuse. She also told me not to be surprised when they wouldn't want to meet with me.

That is exactly what they did. I kept calling trying to set up a time to meet with them, and each time they said no. They had never told us not to come and visit before now, so they knew what was coming. Janice finally told me to just show up at their house and talk to them that way. So, James and I picked a day, had Sue watch our children, and drove to Wisconsin where they were living. God gave me strength as we knocked on the door.

Father answered and was not happy to see us. He started to close the door with the "now is not a great time" excuse, and I put my foot in the door. "Father, we are going to have to do this sometime. We might as well get it over with."

With a big sigh, he opened the door. We were not taken to the cozy family room, but to the stuffy, formal living room. Mother came through the door and when I hugged her she was as rigid as stone. Her arms did not hug me; she was totally cold. I knew that the talk was not going to go well.

I started by telling them all the good things they had done for me in my life and how much I appreciated it. Then, I told them what I had been going through, and that I remembered Father molesting me.

"See," he said, turning to Mother. "I told you this is what it was all about." He turned to me. "But don't twist that against me. I never did anything to you."

I talked to them about being very young and telling Mother that he was hurting me in my private area and Mother remembered no such thing. I talked about the things she had said in previous phone conversations. She replied that she would "never" have said any of them. Things got tenser by the moment. As Father was talking, his lips curled into a sneer as he finished his thought with "...and as you put it, molested you."

That was when I got angry. His denial was one thing, but everyone in the room now knew what he had done. For him to smirk at me was more than I could take. I took the notes I had brought with me and slammed them on the end table.

"Don't call it that!" I yelled, "Call it what it is. You raped me!"

Father's face turned puce and he started coming out of the chair in a threatening manner. James jumped up and put himself between me and Father.

"Get out of my house!" The bellow was deep and we did just that.

I had naively thought he would cry and apologize, and everything could be fixed. But that is not what happened; it was a defining moment in so many ways. It caused a permanent separation and my children would never again see their grandparents.

Mother and Father immediately stopped sending my children cards and gifts, and all phone calls stopped. Yet, I knew that it was time to stand up for myself and tell Father what he did was wrong. I had to confront it. I could no longer keep silent.

There was something terrifying about facing my parents with the truth, yet there was also a freedom and strength that came with my experience. Very few sexual abuse victims have their abusers admit to what they had done. Leaving my parents' house that day, never to return, erased the feeling that I was a victim. Never would Father have power over me again. James and I would protect our children.

The next day, we were at church expecting James' parents. Tim and Sue were very late for the service. After the service, I asked Sue why they were late. She and Tim said that my parents had called them that morning trying to convince them that I was lying. Both Sue and Tim courageously and graciously told my parents that they believed me and would help them get the help they needed. Father was furious and hung up on them. I was in shock! My parents were on the offensive; I didn't even know there was a war.

Father was in attack mode, and he was just getting started. My current pastor informed me that Father had contacted him to tell him of my accusations and that I was emotionally unstable. Thankfully, we had a small church and my pastor knew me better than that.

The next step in the attack became evident when I started getting letters from my aunts, uncles, and cousins on Father's side of the family. They told me how wrong I was, what a horrible daughter I was, and how their kids would never accuse them of such a thing. One aunt even told me that she had grown up sleeping in the same bed as Father until he got married. She said he had never done anything to her.

I was so embarrassed that he had shared my abuse with my relatives. I was now forced to be on the defensive with my own extended family. What had happened to the large, wonderful family I had grown up in? I thought my aunts and uncles loved me, but that love was quickly replaced with animosity. Having my family turn on me hurt me terribly. I had lost my family which was, other than God, my great love and passion.

Psalm 55:12-14

For it was not an enemy that reproached me; then I could have borne it: neither was it he that hated me that did magnify himself against me; then I would have hid myself from him: But it was thou, a man mine equal, my guide, and mine acquaintance. We took sweet counsel together, and walked unto the house of God in company. (KJV)

Song

"When the Tears Fall"
Tim Hughes (Hughs, 2004)

The Cost

The cost can't be counted
I pay as I go
It continues to climb
I continue to owe

He runs up the bills
I pay with my life
He sees me and laughs
I cry at the price

Am I Crazy?

~*~

My breasts were very late in developing. I was the only female in my class not to have a bra and I received a lot of teasing because of it. Yet, my breasts were so painful that I felt like crying if someone just looked at them. Then one day, they started to develop...

It was the middle of the night and Father was furious. As I obediently took off my clothes, his eyes spied my breasts and their small beginnings of development. He exploded with anger as he stood over me on the bed and pressed the palms of his hands against them, leaning down with all the weight he could muster. The pain was searing as I retreated into my eyes and to the left side of my brain.

~*~

After the nightmares and flashbacks began, I was still trying to live the life of a normal wife, mom, and homemaker. My Stephanie was in first grade and we were homeschooling. I was barely able to keep it going. The flashbacks always came when I was fully awake and not expecting them. I would fall apart for days. My nights continued to be filled with the nightmares of being gang raped, and my days were spent in anxious-dread of what I would remember next.

By summer, I had convinced myself that I was going crazy. James and I decided that I needed to go to an outpatient counseling center. On the way, we wanted to see Pastor Molnar, who had been my pastor as a child. He and his wife graciously opened their home to us and were very kind.

I decided that this was a good time to ask questions. Pastor Molnar had known my parents better than most people did. He told me of the time when my mother had taken my brother and me to Wisconsin to visit her family and decided she wasn't going to go back to Father. I remembered that trip. It was the only time we went without Father to Wisconsin, and the only time we stayed a month. I was probably eleven at the time. When we came home, there was a yellow bow tied around our oak tree, and a brand-new microwave in the kitchen. Father never bought gifts, so this was a big deal. At the time, I remember thinking, "Wow, they must have had a big fight."

Pastor Molnar said that when my mother got back, he asked her why she had left. She told him that Father was starting to treat me as badly as he treated her. I was shocked. I couldn't believe that her leaving had been about me.

Father's treatment of me at the time had changed. He yelled at me constantly whether I did anything wrong or not. He would accuse me of horrible motives that just weren't true. He humiliated me in front of other people. It made no sense that he had such rage aimed at me. I was always an obedient daughter and had tried very hard to please everyone.

Pastor Molnar looked thoughtful and said, "Now I know why your parents left my church. I was beginning to counsel women who had been sexually abused and started to talk about it from the pulpit. That is exactly when your family left."

I had never been given a reason why we left Pastor Molnar's church. The only instructions given were to never talk with him or his family again. Leaving the church was a blow. I had learned so much about God during the seven years we had been there, and suddenly I had no one to teach me about the Bible. I remember telling my parents that I felt like I was losing everything I had learned about God. Father ended up yelling at me, telling me that growing in God was my own responsibility. I was fourteen years old.

During our visit, Pastor Molnar and his wife helped me understand more about my life. It was shocking and I was left stunned when more pieces were put together. My courageous and ever faithful James drove me to the facility and returned home to watch over the children. I would be at the clinic for two weeks.

A resident psychiatrist at the clinic was extremely helpful. As I talked about what had happened to me, the flashbacks, the emotions, the pieces of the puzzle I had found, the psychiatrist validated the process and explained to me how abuse worked. He said "my mother and brothers believed Father over me. If they had been able to believe me, they would have stopped the abuse long ago." The doctor explained "It takes a family of people shutting their eyes for abuse to happen, and when the victim talks about the abuse, the family members have to shun the victim." That was certainly what happened.

I experienced my first panic attack at the clinic. I was in a group session, and a woman started talking about being sexually abused by her father. Even though her abuse was different in many ways, my heart started racing with the fight or flight instinct and I ran out of the room with no destination at all. I just knew I had to get away.

The secretary grabbed my arm as I ran by, steering me into a conference room, and got a counselor. After calming me down, the counselor explained what a panic attack was and why it had happened. The woman had hit upon what happened to me, which caused my entire body to panic. Unfortunately, it was the first of many panic attacks that I would have through the years. My body always knew so much more about the abuse than I did. It remembered every detail.

The two weeks at the clinic taught me a lot. One counselor said, "A person can't hold emotions down forever. It's like holding a beach ball under water. You can do it for a while, but then it will eventually get heavier and heavier, until it pops out. The same is true for a person who tries to minimize their emotions. You cannot block out a single emotion; it would cause all the others to shut down also."

This understanding helped to explain my emotional state the summer before the memories came out. It was a season of a complete emotion shutdown. I was emotionally numb with no explanation as to why. Here I was, living a fairytale life with a wonderful husband whom I adored and three amazing children. We had just built and moved into our dream house and I should have felt happy; instead, I felt nothing. Now, I understood the numbing and the "ball of terror feelings" that would try to surface and bubble out. My emotions and trauma were my beach ball.

Psalm 37:1-7

Fret not thyself because of evildoers, neither be thou envious against the workers of iniquity. For they shall soon be cut down like the grass, and wither as the green herb. Trust in the Lord, and do good; so shalt thou dwell in the land, and verily thou shalt be fed. Delight thyself also in the Lord: and he shall give thee the desires of thine heart. Commit thy way unto the Lord; trust also in him; and he shall bring it to pass. And he shall bring forth thy righteousness as the light, and thy judgment as the noonday. Rest in the Lord, and wait patiently for him: fret not thyself because of him who prospereth in his way, because of the man who bringeth wicked devices to pass. (KJV)

Song

"Lord I Give You My Heart"
Michael W. Smith (Morgan, 2002)

A Note from Pastor Molnar

~*~

Where do I begin? I'm at a loss for words after reading your galley proof "Only God Rescued Me." I had to stop several times in the reading for the weeping over you in what you were facing. Then, as I begin to write something out for you, I had to stop and weep for the pain and suffering you had endured. My weeping was not only for the things you were experiencing, but also for the fact that I didn't know what you were going through and not able to help stop it.

Next came the tears of joy as I was reminded of the fact that you are on the other side of it all, being healed and blessed by the power of God. You survived the abuse and were able to grow in Faith and in Love standing on the Word of God that was planted in the good, rich soil of your heart.

Knowing you as a young girl, seeing your sweet smile, the purity of your heart and the love of the Lord God had never diminished although your body, the flesh, was attacked, abused, and defiled. Because your spirit was so in union with, connected, and filled with the Holy Spirit, you were able to defeat Satan's plans and designs. At this juncture, it is important to know and understand that you are not a mere survivor, YOU ARE AN OVERCOMER, MORE THAN A CONQUERER! You have persevered, pressed on and OVERCOME the vilest and wicked devilish attacks. You didn't succumb to the will of evil but prevailed by the Power of "Almighty God!" That is because your passion was to love the Lord your God with all your heart, with all your soul, and with all your mind.

I do remember sharing the Word of God with you at your home on several occasions. I'm not sure of your age, I think about twelve. One of the times you were sitting on the piano bench with full attention to what I was teaching. You were so hungry for the Word of God. It seemed that the truth of the Bible was so important to you. Your desire seemed to increase. I recall the first time you came to the Wednesday night Bible study and had a Bible and a note pad. You actually took notes of the messages. I noticed how intense you were to learn. You were the only young person in an adult audience. At times I would ask questions pertaining to the teaching and you were very quick to respond with the correct answer. You really inspired me to teach and preach the Word of God. I know that many of the messages and teachings I gave were with you in mind at that time not knowing how important that would become in your life. Some adults were only physically there, while you were so spiritually aware, open and hungry for the truths in the Word of God. You were like a dry sponge; the Word of God was like fresh water coming over you. You soaked it up, not letting any of it flow away. As I think back on those times, I never have had anyone, youth or adult, before or since, demonstrate such a strong desire and craving for the Word of God as you had.

Then many years later I became aware of you dealing with the major issues of abuse and my heart was so broken for you. I have admired your courage and strength to continue to grow, be delivered, and healed of the past. What a joy it has been to counsel and pray with you and see the wonderful recovery you have made. As you continue to seek the Lord God Almighty to fulfill His will in your life, I'm reminded of two scriptures:

Philippians 1:6
Being confident of this very thing, that He which hath began a good work in you will perform it until the day of Jesus Christ. (KJV)

Psalms 138:8
The Lord will perfect (mature, fulfill, complete) that which concerneth me. (KJV)

I can very well imagine how proud the Lord is of you. You are an OVERCOMER, A CONQUEROR! I know how proud I am of your Faith and your Love of the Lord and His Word. I'm so blessed to know you and have you as a dear friend all these years. The Lord is really going to use you to be an inspiration and blessing to many victims and survivors. I close with this most fitting verse that the Apostle Paul shared with the believers in:

2 Corinthians 1: 3-4
Blessed be God, even the Father of our Lord Jesus Christ, the Father of mercies, and the God of all comfort; who comforteth us in our tribulation, that we may be able to comfort them which are in any trouble, by the comfort wherewith we ourselves are comforted of God. (KJV)

With all my Love, Prayers, and Blessings,
Pastor Clifford Molnar

There Is Pain Inside

There is pain inside, you cannot see
It locks me up
In great misery

The pain it grows, it growls and snares
I hear the scream
My terror shares

My body tells, about this pain
It drives my doctors
Quite insane

It tried to keep, from getting out
Under wraps
Then I could doubt

But the pain was smart, it over me rolled
I got no vote
My tale was told

I gasp and wheeze, roll in pain
Toilet hug
Throbbing migraine

In the past, my thoughts suspend
Will the suffering
Never end

But in between, here and there
I find a day
With health to spare

~*~

Now I Know I'm Crazy

~*~

I was very young and completely naked on top of a table. Each limb was tied to a corner of the table. The room was black with candles, smoke, and chanting. A robed figure with a hood obscuring his face spread peanut butter in a cross like shape across my chest and from neck down to my private area. I was terrified, but not able to move or communicate. All I wanted was to get home to my bed and hug my Raggedy Ann. Robed figures brought mice over, holding them in their hands, and let them loose on my body. I felt their claws scratch me as they ran around my body and ate the peanut butter. I saw them bring over a cat and let it loose on the table, catching one of the mice. The cat sat on my chest with the mouse hanging out of its mouth. My body slowly disappeared and I was just my eyes. I didn't like seeing the cat and mouse, so I receded even further into my brain.

~*~

After my two weeks at the clinic, I went back home and once again tried to focus on taking care of homeschooling, kids, husband, and house. Getting anything done was difficult. It had been nine months since the dinner with my parents, and I seemed to be getting worse, not better. Feelings of terror were starting to take over. Summer turned into fall, always my worst time of year for as long as I could remember. Every year I fell apart for the entire season. Halloween terrified me, and James always got me out of the house so I didn't have to deal with trick-or-treaters.

One day I felt scratching all over the top part of my body. It was horrible, like my nerve endings had just completely fritzed out. This wasn't anything like the flashbacks I had had until now. I took a soft blanket and just kept rubbing it over my body and took lots of Advil to try to get rid of the feeling. Nothing worked. After a few days, I had the flashback of the mice and cat.

It hit me hard, and I had no idea what it meant. The episode was totally different than the nightmares, flashbacks, and memories of Father's sexual abuse of me. I completely went into hysterics, actually feeling the mice run across my body. I couldn't get rid of it. I had no idea where I was and I couldn't figure out why I was tied down. It just didn't make sense, and again, my mind was tormented by what my body seemed to remember.

How in the world would I tell James about this? I had no idea what it was, so how could I explain it? There was no context, just the one scene. If James didn't find me disgusting before, he definitely would now. Besides, I didn't believe that this had actually happened to me as a child. I was convinced more than ever that I was losing my mind.

I cried hysterically, curled into a fetal position on my bed. The option to keep it from James disappeared when he came into our bedroom with love and concern in his eyes. He held me while I sobbed.

I found myself unable to speak what I had seen in my mind's eye and experienced in my physical body. I grabbed paper and pencil and wrote down the flashback, if that was what it was. I handed the paper to James and watched his face carefully as he read it. His face grew pale and he looked up at me. I carefully explained that this experience was proof that I was crazy, because there was no way it could be a real memory of what actually happened to me as a child. James assured me that he loved me and that we would figure this out together.

I am still shocked that he believed me that day. He told me that it sounded like something called ritual abuse. I had heard the phrase, but had no idea what it meant. Neither did James. We held each other, feeling lost and confused. The past ten months had been rough, but the future was looking even darker.

After the flashback of the cat and mice, the memories came in quick succession. There were people in black robes with hoods that completely covered their faces. There were candles, smoke, chanting, bonfires, tables, rape, gang rape, killing, and demonic sounding voices. I refused to believe it. But the flashbacks wouldn't stop. I had pain and sensations in a part of my body, with no idea where that feeling could possibly have come from, only to have the flashback hit a few days later that showed exactly how the pain got there. As much as I really, really, really wanted to just throw it out and not deal with it, I realized I had no control in this process. My body was telling me its story and I was the captive audience.

The only person I felt I could trust with these new horrific flashbacks was the psychiatrist at the outpatient clinic I had gone to. James and I packed up the kids and went back to the clinic. We went in and I told the psychiatrist everything that I was remembering and experiencing. I told him every humiliating thing, and I really hoped that he would tell me that I was crazy. In my mind it would be much easier to deal with being crazy than having to believe the flashbacks truly happened to me.

The psychiatrist waited until I was done talking, and then told me that he already knew that I had been ritualistically abused. My jaw was on the floor. He explained that the level of severity of the sexual abuse was in the top 90th percentile. He said people only get to that degree through being involved in ritual abuse. He gave a small presentation of what SRA (Satanic Ritual Abuse) was and its history. He assured me that this had happened to many children, but the public didn't want to believe it and refused to listen to survivors. Survivors were attacked, humiliated, and considered to be liars. This would not be an easy group of which to be a part.

As the reality of SRA settled in, I felt like I needed to go back to where I had grown up to see if I could find "proof" that I really was a survivor of ritual abuse. Actually, I was looking more for proof that it didn't happen. I felt torn. Everything inside of me was accepting the truth of SRA while my mind was in a constant whirl trying to find the best strategy to disprove it.

We packed up the kids and Sue to go back to the town I grew up in. When we arrived, we stayed with friends while I tried to figure out what to do. My mind was completely blank as to what to do to accomplish this task. I prayed and waited to know how I was going to do this. Finally I felt led to find a woman who had worked with Father for many years. Father was a pharmacist and owned his own pharmacy. She had spent a lot of time working with him, and she was the one I felt I needed to talk to.

I called Catherine and told her why I wanted to speak with her, and she invited us over. Catherine, Sue, James and I sat at her kitchen table while the kids were noisily playing around her living room, having a lot of fun. Watching the children, Catherine said, "I am so thrilled to see your kids like this!"

"What do you mean?" I asked.

"When you were that age, and you and your brothers came with Father to visit, you would sit on the couch and not move or talk unless he gave you permission. He even told me that you would not think for yourself until you were in college."

I thought about this and how Father insisted on controlling me. When I had found out what abortion was and spoke about how horrible it was, Father angrily told me not to give an opinion about something I didn't know anything about. When I was in college I got angry letters for not taking his advice as to what I should or should not do on campus. Catherine was right.

"He also complained about your mother a lot, because she was always sick." Mother struggled with colitis and a partially lame leg from a botched surgery. Catherine said Father complained about how horrible it was for a man not to be able to be intimate with his wife very often. Catherine said Father had made sexual advances towards her and told us she had had to quit working with him because of it. We thanked Catherine and I left with a heavy load. My talk with Catherine helped me put even more pieces of my puzzled past together.

I had been thinking of the witch Father had taken me to as a child and wondered about her identity. I met again with Pastor Molnar and asked him about her. Pastor Molnar said that before my parents started going to his church, they were involved in witchcraft. Father told Pastor Molnar he had seen the power of the devil but he didn't see such power from God.

We also learned that the previous pastor had a son who had been found having sex with the city's acclaimed witch on the altar of the church. This was a big scandal in a small town, and the pastor had to leave.

I was able to find the name of the witch, and because she was living in another state, we tracked down her ex-husband. James and I went to his house and knocked on the door. His current wife answered the door. I recognized her as a past customer of Father's pharmacy. I had worked at the pharmacy from the ages of eleven to twenty, so I knew the customers and they knew me.

She recognized who I was and I told her we would like to talk to her husband. She let us in and her heavyset husband was sulking at the small kitchen table. I told him my maiden name and explained I used to work for Father at his pharmacy downtown. He immediately looked at James with something like fear in his eyes. He told me he didn't know the pharmacy. That was an obvious lie and everyone in the room knew it because of how small the town was. His wife told him that he did know the pharmacy. Again he denied it. Finally his wife disappeared and came back into the room carrying a bookmark with the name of Father's pharmacy printed on it. The bookmark was soiled from a lot of use. She put it on the table in front of him and he just stared at it. There was nothing he could refute at that point.

Strategy suggested that I stop pushing him on a stupid lie and talk to him about his ex-wife, who had been known around town as a witch. We had found her daughter in the phone book, and she told us some spooky things about her mom. I explained to the witch's ex-husband about how I knew that he and the witch had been part of a group Father had been involved in. He didn't deny it, just looked at me warily. Finally, he told us he didn't go to the rituals with her much, but the witch had gone a lot.

I asked him if he ever saw children being abused in any way in that group. He once again looked at James, as if to gauge what James' reaction would be. Then he completely denied any children being involved. Although he denied the children being involved, he did validate my parents being in the same group with the witch.

I really didn't want to know any more information on what Father had been up to, so I told James that I was ready to go. We went back home and I tried to add up all the information I had just learned with the information I had prior to the trip.

I remembered my parents being part of what they called a "new age" group when they were "searching for truth." They would send me and my brothers into the basement so they could meditate. I was young, so I asked Mother what it meant. She told me that it was being very quiet and thinking about nothing. I went to the basement to try to mediate as well. I sat on an upturned bucket and tried to clear my mind. I could only think about not thinking, so finding it stupid, I commenced playing with the toys we had down there.

Another piece I could collect was a memory of a bizarre English teacher at the community college I attended my senior year in high school. When students exhausted the high school curriculum at our small school, the school board paid to send the students to the community college to get dual credits. I took an English class the first semester and had a big, burly man with a bushy, black beard and missing a leg. He would roll around the room in his wheelchair during the class when he was lecturing. He loved to roll to a stop where I sat, which was always as far to the back and as far away from him as possible. As he was lecturing, he would lean into my personal space and terrify me. He never did this to anyone else. One day I mentioned it to Father and Mother and they laughed when I told them the name of the professor. They told me that he was part of the "new age" group that they had been a part of. I did not find it funny at all.

As I started piecing together what I had learned along with the ever worsening flashbacks, I made a decision. As much as I wanted all this to be wrong, I decided to not fight it. I had fought the memories with every bit of energy I had so this was a big strategy change. I had no idea what I was in for.

Psalm 91:4-5

He shall cover thee with his feathers, and under his wings shalt thou trust: his truth shall be thy shield and buckler. Thou shalt not be afraid for the terror by night. (KJV)

Song

"Just Be Held"
Casting Crowns (Crowns, Just Be Held)

Memories

Regretful days
Of decades past
Terror nights
Abuse surpassed

Stinging still
Inside my heart
Crushing weight
Oh pain depart

Striving leave
It all behind
Nightmares stay
Plight in mind

Each and every
Single night
Why must stay
Please take flight

I have wrestled
With each fear
Husband held
Wiped each tear

Will it ever
Be enough
Aren't I here
Because am tough

If I be strong
Then go away
I will not wrestle
You today
~*~

The Lawyer

It was dark and I was standing at the top edge of a deep grave. By moonlight, I could see what appeared to be a teenage girl with dark hair and a ponytail down in the freshly dug hole. Her body was posed as if it had been dumped into the grave from above. I was encircled with faceless, black robed people. A man with a deep, chilling voice behind me was saying that "the girl had told." He reached his arms around me, grabbed my hands, and put them around a huge butcher knife. I was in my eyes as he showed me how to stick the blade under my breast bone and thrust upward into my heart. I was then handed a shovel and told to fill in the grave. My head was invisibly shaking "no". I just couldn't force myself to do it. A hand came over my mouth and nose so that I could not breathe. When the dark tunnel started to form, the hand came off allowing me to gasp for air. I was again ordered to fill the grave in and I did. My brain disconnected from my hands as I obeyed. The night seemed to go on forever.

I spent the next three months on the couch crying in terror. Any sound would make me jump. I was sure that the cult had caught up with me and would kill me and my family. I would literally crawl into the kitchen to try to find something to feed the children. I was hopeless with dread and convinced that this fear would never go away. By this time, I had another counselor who'd never counseled a Satanic Ritual Abuse survivor before me. I soon came to the realization that I was a survivor of SRA. My counselor helped me through the flashbacks, using various coping methods to survive each new memory. But survival was as far as we got.

The amount of energy it took for me to keep going was monumental. I was beyond exhausted. It took all the strength I had to keep the kids homeschooled, fed, and clothed. Dinner was often too much for me to handle, so James would bring something home for us to eat or he would grill us up hamburgers and hotdogs. Laundry became mountains of unfolded, clean clothes. Housework was minimal; toys were everywhere. James asked to have a path cleared when he came home and that is pretty much all he had.

Pouring my heart out to God was the only thing that kept me going. I soon realized that He was the only reason I had survived this process. I also came to realize that God had been there with me through every ritual. He was the only one that knew it all. He had never turned away from me, although I would have preferred that He would've sent a physical person to rescue me. Looking back, I now see that the rescue was in the long haul. Spiritually, I had survived the abuse. God never let go of me.

As autumn turned into winter, my parents continued to be in attack mode. I got a letter from my grandfather via registered mail. My mother's parents were frugal, making a hard living at dairy farming and producing milk. Paying extra money to send a registered letter didn't go along with how they lived, so I knew something was up.

The letter was filled with all the different reasons why I should be ashamed of myself for the pain that I was causing my "dear mother." Grandpa advised that I give this up and come back into the family. I was crushed. Family had always been of great importance to me, and he never even asked me for my side of what happened.

I decided to phone my grandparents. Grandpa and Grandma got on the phone. I tried to tell them what Father had done to me and Grandpa stopped me. He didn't want to hear anything about it.

He reiterated some of his thoughts that he had sent in the letter. When I asked him why he had sent the letter via registered mail, he explained that my mother had told him I wasn't receiving my mail. James' dad was intercepting it before it reached me, so no letters were getting through. I asked him if he had sent a letter that I hadn't received and he mumbled a soft "no." I explained to my grandpa that this was not true, and that I could take a video of me getting my own mail every day if he wanted me too. This seemed to fluster him and he quickly ended the call.

Grandpa and I had precious few phone calls through the years; he never would listen to what had happened to me. In the end, he just didn't care. He wanted the family to look good even if it was dangerously broken.

Numerous other lies my extended family told seemed to always find their way back to me. Father and Mother were telling people that James and Sue had put these thoughts of abuse into my head. They told people that I was a prisoner in my own home and at that point, I got really angry! My parents' denial could only work if they lied about me, but lying about the two people who were standing by my side through all my suffering made me so mad. I was determined that this had to be stopped!

I decided to go to a Christian lawyer to see if there was anything James and I could do to stop the lies. I explained about the sexual abuse at home and the SRA. I figured the lawyer would have to believe everything or nothing. The fear of not being believed was very strong.

The lawyer listened, jotting notes on his pad of paper. When I finished, he sat for a few moments and collected his thoughts. He kindly explained that there wasn't anything he could do about the lies the relatives were spreading. My heart sunk. I realized how naïve it had been for me to think that a lawyer could stop what was happening. He went on and explained that I had the right to either press criminal charges or sue my parents. He felt I had more than enough evidence to win either.

Wow! I was shocked. The idea that no one would believe me had been ingrained by the cult, yet here… not only was I believed, my story was validated in knowing that I could file a legal case and probably win.

The lawyer asked what expenses we had incurred because of the abuse, and James and I had to think. The bills were already steep. There was counseling not covered by insurance, the outpatient clinic that I had stayed at for two weeks, countless take–out meals, lots of food that had spoiled when I could not cook, and having to hire help with the major cleaning of our house. It added up to a lot of money, but how do you put a dollar figure on what I had gone through?

My lawyer suggested that I write Father a letter asking him for $10,000 to cover the expenses of the abuse. That made sense. He should be the one financially responsible for the damage he had done to me.

I wrote the letter to Father asking for the money. I kept it brief and to the point. He and I both knew what he had done, so I wasn't playing any games pretending that he did not know. I told him that he abused me and it was costing a lot of money for recovery. Would he send $10,000 to cover the expenses?

A week later, I received a bouquet of flowers. It came to the door with a card that said, "Love, Father." This was his response to my letter. I took the bouquet to the kitchen and began pulling the petals off one by one. My two – year old wandered into the kitchen and decided that pulling off petals looked like fun. She helped me until we had pulled all the flowers apart. I was so angry that his reply was flowers.

Up until this point, I had been against filing charges against Father, yet I felt God wanting me to do just that. I really, really didn't want to do it. I had His assurance that He would be with me.

Revealing my past to law enforcement would take me to a whole new level of courage. My abuse was horrible to admit to myself and it took months to admit it to James. After that, we went to his parents. Then there were pastors and family members, friends... What I had naively thought was a private matter was no longer a secret. Finding an attorney and telling him was a big step, going to the police would be entirely different situation. It terrified me to even think about talking to the police.

Pursuing the legal avenue meant that Father could end up in prison. I wasn't sure what I wanted for him. Did I want him in prison for what he did to me? He certainly deserved it. Did I want to be known in public as a survivor of SRA? Would my family be safe? If I couldn't handle counseling sessions, how in the world would I handle court? What if no one believed me or the prosecutor wasn't able to prove it?

In the end, the decision came down to doing what God had told me to do. My life's motto had always been, "If God tells you to do something, do it, even if you don't understand it." Either I trust God in everything, or I trust Him in nothing at all.

Through prayer and soul searching, I realized that Father was still free to harm others. If he were in prison there would be no opportunity. The sexual abuse books I had read said, "Perpetrators don't quit and have many victims over the years." That meant there were more children Father was hurting. I knew that he had to be stopped.

Proverbs 5:21

For the ways of man are before the eyes of the LORD, and he pondereth all his goings.

Isaiah 55:8-9

For my thoughts are not your thoughts, neither are your ways my ways, saith the Lord, for as the heavens are higher than the earth, so are my ways higher than your ways, and my thoughts than your thoughts. (KJV)

Song

"Mighty to Save"
Hillsong (Fielding & Morgan, 2006)

Justice vs. Revenge

I struggled with the concept of justice and revenge. I felt God strongly leading me to go to the police and press charges against Father, yet it was extremely hard to do because he was, after all, still my father. No matter how wicked and twisted the abuse was, a part of me was still the little girl trying to see her father as perfect.

It made no sense to me and finally, my psychiatrist helped me to understand. "Revenge would be doing to Father what he did to me." There was no way that I would ever want a person to endure what I had gone through. It also occurred to me that even if the same abuse was done to Father, it would not have the same impact on an adult as it did a child. Some could argue if Father had actually been subjected to this kind of abuse as a child (and was a victim himself), that he should not be held accountable. To this, I disagree.

The moment Father started abusing other children he chose to align himself with the abusers and became one himself. Although the likelihood was high that he was a victim also, I would have no way of knowing for certain that he had ever been abused.

Justice is very different. It suggests a following of governmental laws. We live in the United States of America where justice is not allowed to be "cruel or unusual." Justice would involve the process of pressing charges, an investigation, a court to determine guilt or innocence, and an appropriate sentencing and jail time.

Going through with pressing charges was terrifying. I realized over time that Father would never contact me for fear that the investigation would be used against him. I also contacted Detective McGowen and explained my fear that the cult would come and kill me or one of my family members. He told me not to worry. If anything happened to me, he would know where to look. At the time, it was not a comfort, but I saw the wisdom in it later. If anything happened to me after pressing charges, the cult would be exposed.

Pressing Charges

~*~

Father came into my room in the middle of the night and told me to take my nightgown off. As always, I did as I was told. But when he told me to open my legs, something inside of me snapped and I held them together as tightly as I could. Tonight, I wasn't going to give in. He got up and I thought he would leave. Instead, he went through my dresser drawers and came back with a pair of socks. He shoved them deep in my mouth. The socks were in too far and I struggled to breathe and not throw up. Meanwhile, with shirts and nightgowns, he tied my hands to the opposite ends of my bed. He jumped on me and told me if I ever did that again, he would kill me. I knew that he was telling the truth. He roughly forced my legs open and raped me more viciously than he ever had before. As the pain ripped me apart, I escaped to the top left of my brain. When it was all over, he untied me and I had no fight left. He sat with tissues wiping the blood from my vagina until the bleeding stopped.

~*~

My lawyer explained to me that there was only a small chance that a district attorney would take on my SRA case. The first step would involve talking with the district attorney in the county where the abuse had happened. Whether or not the D.A. would try the case would depend solely on if the district attorney believed in the current practice of SRA or felt that she could win the case. It would also depend on the district attorney's caseload. Since it had happened in a small town in Minnesota, the chances were that the D.A.'s office was understaffed.

With this understanding, I called my attorney and told him that I had decided to file criminal charges. My lawyer contacted the district attorney in Minnesota and I waited on pins and needles to hear what the D.A. had decided. Even with all the amazing people who had believed that I was an SRA survivor, I was still convinced that the District Attorney would not. Ironically, there were times I did not believe it myself, but that's how the mind of an SRA survivor works.

When the District Attorney's office bravely took the case, (SRA and all) I could not believe it. The D.A. said someone would be in contact with me soon. That someone turned out to be Detective McGowen.

James and I lived nine hours from the county where the abuse had occurred. Surprisingly, the detective was coming through our state and scheduled to stop to talk with us and record the information of what had happened to me. Before he came through town, I had one more chance to go to my parents and see if they were willing to deal with the abuse. If not, I would be talking to the detective.

I believed it was only right to give Father one more opportunity to admit to the abuse and get help before I formally talked with Detective McGowen. All Father had to do was admit what he had done and get therapy. That was what I had wanted to happen all along. The Bible tells us that if we have a problem with someone we are to go and try to work it out, which James and I had already done. The next step is to take someone to be a witness when you talk to them for the second time. This is what I felt James and I needed to do.

We had a new pastor at our church by this time. We shared everything that was going on in our healing process with Pastor Sluzas and asked if he would help facilitate a meeting between my parents, their pastor, James, and me. The courage that Pastor Sluzas had to walk into our mess never ceased to amaze me. He traveled all the way just to be with us and arranged a private meeting with my parent's pastor beforehand.

I told Pastor Baker, Father and Mother's pastor, the details of my past including the SRA. After listening, he said that he believed me. He shared that there was always something about Father that didn't seem right. He did not understand what he was discerning until a member of the church who was spiritually attuned came to him and warned him of Father, saying, "There is something really evil in him."

Pastor Baker said the woman had never done this before, so he was more apt to take note of what she had discerned. He also told us that my parents were teaching an elementary Sunday school class and he would relieve them of this position. We set a date for the pastors, my parents, and all of us to meet.

The meeting was set and again Pastor Sluzas bravely accompanied us. This was the first time I had seen my parents in a year. They ignored James and me as we walked into the church until they saw other church people in the office. Then they made a big show of greeting us and looking hurt when we wouldn't let them hug us. Seeing them again made me feel frozen and I dissociated, going into just my eyes. When Mother approached me to hug me, my head did the minimal shaking back and forth in a "no." Soon we were all ushered into the office.

Pastor Sluzas prayed first, allowing me time to fight my way back into the present. Thankfully, I had a list of questions for Father to answer. The questions were designed to let me know if he was going to be truthful and admit to what he had done. I was determined not to respond to any of his answers, but to just hear them. My goal was only to see Father's intentions, and I forced myself to stick with the plan.

I was determined to focus and stay on track, not engage. This helped me to stay in the present moment. Interestingly enough, I realized that Father was the one dissociating. He was staring off into a certain place like he wasn't there in the room with us. I suddenly realized that he had done this my entire life, I just never noticed it before. I knew the likelihood of abuse in our home and SRA came generationally through Father. What I did not understand at that time was that generational SRA accounts for almost all of its members. There was a high probability that Father had also been victimized.

Father quickly went into attack mode. Still, I was able to keep my focus. When he began to insult me, I stopped for a moment, choking off the retort I wanted to give. I told him that we could insult each other, but it would accomplish nothing. I calmly informed him that I had contacted the District Attorney in our home county, and had talked to a detective about the sexual abuse in our home. I also shared the SRA in detail with the D.A. If he wasn't willing to admit his abuse and engage in therapy, the next step was for me to press charges against him.

Father sneered. "I won't admit to anything! The District Attorney will never take on the case!" I lifted my brow and informed him that the D.A. had already taken the case and was waiting for the go-ahead. I could see fear in Father's eyes. Within moments it changed to seething anger. I could tell that he was barely able to control it. This was the same look of rage that he had worn when he violently raped me. I knew that he would not concede.

There was no longer a reason to continue the talk. Father wouldn't admit to the abuse or ask for help, so the meeting ended. We drove home processing and trying to find out what direction we were to go next. One thing was clear, it was time for me to go on the offensive.

Detective McGowen was on his way to our house to hear what I had to say. I was terrified to meet the officer. I cleaned the house with a vengeance. Everything had such an eerie feeling about it. I felt that if anything was out of place in my house, he would not believe me. By the time he arrived, I had worked myself into an emotional wreck. However, Detective McGowen was very kind and I instantly felt at ease speaking with him.

I wrung my hands as I told him about the sexual abuse that had occurred at the hands of Father. He gently probed with questions and I answered them, all the while wondering what he was thinking. Soon it was time to take the plunge, and I told him about the SRA. I was sure he would not believe me, but I was completely honest. He listened very carefully, taking notes, and asking questions here and there. When I finished, I waited in fear for what he was going to say.

Detective McGowen told me that a year ago he wouldn't have believed me, but then he was assigned a case where a teenager had disappeared. Some were convinced that a Satanic Ritual Cult had killed her. This had caused him to delve deep into the existence of SRA. Eventually, he found the teen who had run away and brought her home safe, but not before he was convinced that his district of Minnesota had SRA cults operating in the region.

During the interview, I mentioned that growing up I never wanted to kiss. I was absolutely terrified of it. The detective asked me if anyone knew how I felt about kissing, since that was an abnormal fear for a teenager. I told him that Kendal, an attorney in the area knew, and had jokingly asked my bridesmaid to check and see if I had actually kissed James at the altar when we married.

Detective McGowen stared at me in a strange way. I was puzzled. There weren't that many lawyers in the county, so he should have known Kendal. (I reasoned that this was the explanation for his strange look.) I asked him if he knew Kendal. He looked me in the eyes and told me that he knew him. I told the detective that Kendal wouldn't know of my intent to press charges against Father.

"Oh, he knows," said Detective McGowen. He lifted his brow and nodded.

I was completely confused. "How would he know?" I asked.

"Lisa, he has been tapping sources at the police department and looking for your statement to see if charges have been filed against your father."

"But why?" I asked.

"Because your father hired him."

I started to shrink into myself and become my eyes. Detective McGowen must have noticed, because he immediately assured me that I was safe and did not have to worry. Knowing that Kendal made the statement about me kissing my husband at the altar was to our benefit. The DA could now call him as a witness. He, then, would not be able to represent Father.

Although that line of reasoning made me feel somewhat better, I felt completely betrayed by Kendal. He had been a youth leader in a Christian group I attended in high school and I still considered him a friend. I could not wrap my head around the fact that Kendal had allowed Father to hire him and had never called to ask me what had happened. The whole concept of him working for Father made me feel sick to my stomach.

I next told Detective McGowen that I was suicidal during my teenage years. I was the babysitter for an attorney in the area for a few years and whenever the he would take me home late and night and was speeding down the road, I would have to fight the urge to open the door and jump out. I literally dug my fingernails into the seat under me to keep myself from actually doing just that. Detective McGowen asked the name of the lawyer. I told him and he got that funny look again and told me that the attorney was now a judge in the county.

I was stunned. How in the world could this be happening? I couldn't go before a judge that I had known, and share what had happened to me! He knew our family.

The detective once again advised me not to worry. The judge would likely recuse himself if my case went to trial. He knew me at the time of the abuse and would be required to step aside. I still felt dejected. I knew the process would be difficult, but this was already insane. "We will handle this one step at a time, Lisa," he said. "I will protect your identity as best as possible. Now that the case is open, I will keep you apprised on what is happening with the investigation."

Detective McGowen called a few weeks later to tell me that he was going go to visit my parents and give them an opportunity to respond to my accusations. He kindly called me after and filled me in.

"I showed up unexpectedly at your parents' door late in the evening. Your father answered the door and I told him that I was here to hear his response to the allegations of abusing you. He told me that I had wasted my time because you were lying. I assured your father that I believed what you told me was true, otherwise I wouldn't be here. 'Come back in the morning,' he said. 'I want to talk to a lawyer first.'"

The next morning, the detective showed back up at my parents' house. Father answered the door and told him that his lawyer had advised him not to give a statement. Even though nothing legally came from this confrontation, it made me feel believed and protected. Finally, someone had stood up against Father and the SRA.

Survivors of SRA rarely have people confronting their abusers. Society chooses to pretend it doesn't happen. Some people believe it, but it terrifies them, so they stay far away. Some people are afraid if they get involved with a victim's plight in any way, they or their families will be killed. Survivors do not get "rescued" by the police when they are young, so they do not get the protection they deserve.

When I was young, I always daydreamed of being rescued. Rescued from what I did not know. Because of my repressed memories, I always had the feeling of something being very wrong, I just couldn't put my finger on what it was. Having the police show up on the doorstep of Father's house and stand up to him was amazing. I saw that I was making incredible progress. I believed what had happened to me, vocalized it to others, got the police behind me, and was now validated by the justice system. Others were now standing up to Father.

A Note from Pastor Sluzas

~*~

I was blessed to have been Lisa's pastor some years ago during a pivotal time when painful memories from the past were coming to the forefront in her life. Both she and her husband, as well as their children, were faithful members of our church.

One would be hard pressed to find more "on fire" and loving believers in Jesus Christ than Lisa and her family. It was during this period when Lisa and her husband began a process of opening up to me as their pastor about what had happened to her as a child at the hands of those whom she trusted the most for nurture and protection; her own parents.

During those months when Lisa and James came to me to share and pray, the Holy Spirit led her to confront her parents who were living in another state. They were members in good standing at another church and we knew that this meeting would not be easy. However, something needed to be done.

The moment of truth had come when all parties concerned agreed to come together in the office of her parents' pastor. When this long overdue meeting with her parents finally occurred, it was with Lisa and her husband, Lisa's parents, their pastor, and me. Though the years have passed since that time, (as have a lot of specific memories) several things from that day have stuck with me.

The couple who brought Lisa into this world and who ultimately should have been her protectors, was now sitting across from her steadfastly denying each and every memory that she was sharing of childhood abuse at their hands. They would smile occasionally and deny her every recollection, cloaking their protestations in religious lingo. All the while, I had an uneasy sense deep in my spirit that they were being untruthful and that there was something spiritually heavy about their denials and demeanor. Their Pastor, while trying to mediate and guide the discussion, apparently sided with her parents.

The meeting that day was difficult, but a necessary step toward Lisa's long-term healing in the coming years and her future ministry of healing to others who suffer silently in the aftermath of Satanic Ritual Abuse. It's been her personal relationship with the Lord Jesus Christ that has brought her healing, grace, mercy, and the fullness of joy that Lisa now longs to share with countless others. Yes, it's true; there's victory in Jesus.

Matthew 18:15-17

...if thy brother shall trespass against you, go and tell him his fault between you and him alone: if he shall hear you, thou hast gained thy brother.
But if he will not hear you, then take with you, one or two more, that in the mouth of two or three witnesses every word may be established.
And if he shall neglect to hear them, tell it unto the church: but if he neglects (refuses) to hear the church, let him be unto you as an heathen man and a publican. (KJV)

Ecclesiastes 3:1-8

To everything there is a season, and a time to every purpose under the heaven: A time to be born, and a time to die; a time to plant, and a time to pluck up that which is planted; A time to kill, and a time to heal; a time to break down, and a time to build up; A time to weep, and a time to laugh; a time to mourn, and a time to dance; A time to cast away stones, and a time to gather stones together; a time to embrace, and a time to refrain from embracing; A time to get, and a time to lose; a time to keep, and a time to cast away; A time to rend, and a time to sew; a time to keep silence, and a time to speak; A time to love, and a time to hate; a time of war, and a time of peace. (KJV)

Song

"Overcomer"
Mandisa (Mandisa, 2013)

Not Invited

I stood in front of a huge bonfire. The ever–present table of sacrifice was in front of it, with the priest standing before it, hands outstretched in the air, over his head. I wore a white gown and stood front and center. Being front and center meant you were going to get the worst of whatever was coming. The hooded, faceless priest talked in an evil, sinister, non-human, demonic voice. He yelled out for everyone to love one another, but I was his. The hooded people all around started having sex. I pulled back into my eyes as the priest headed my way. By the time he reached me, I was in my head.

James and I rode the waves of flashbacks and emotions for several months. I fought every memory that tried to come out, trying to push it back down. Each time the pain of the memory yet to come stayed in my body. I would fight against it until I was exhausted, finally allowing it to come. The memories came in strange places: the grocery store, at church in the middle of a sermon, and even when we had company. It got to the point I had so many flashbacks coming that I could no longer deny them.

Life was hard. Not only was I dealing with the memories, which were physically and mentally exhausting, but I had all my normal duties as housewife, mom, and home-school teacher. I was so happy to have the responsibilities of homeschooling. It was something I loved doing, and it forced me to get up in the morning.

I managed homeschooling, but the house slowly fell apart as I got less and less functional. I couldn't follow simple recipes that I had been cooking for years. Many meals had to be pitched and then we would have to go out to eat. Money was tight, but we hired a sweet woman to clean for us. Candi was a godsend. She was so kind and loved on the kids. She not only cleaned, but was also able to straighten up the mess the house had become. Candi was an angel sent to us in our time of need.

I really don't know how James and I got through that time in our lives. He did everything he could to hold me together emotionally. His encouragement gave me strength to look forward. One of the most valuable lessons I learned from James was that I would not be stuck in this torment forever. When something bad was happening, it was easy to think that it would never stop. Over and over James would remind me of God's goodness and assure me that we would make it through this together. I don't think I would have kept my sanity without him.

The presence of God held me through this process. Every day was painful, yet I knew He was with me and walking me through this valley. I held onto knowing that He was a good Father and even in my worst days, He never left me. Scripture after scripture that I had hidden inside my heart would surface during times of despair and bring me peace.

James' parents were also there for me. Whenever I needed to talk, Sue would make time for me. She called daily to check in to see if I was okay. She and Tim, James' father, were available whenever we needed something. There brought over many meals and washed mounds of laundry. I am overwhelmed with thanksgiving when I think of support of James' parents and love through this time. I could never thank them enough for all their help through those years.

One day, I received a wedding invitation from one of my brothers. Within the invitation was a note that I was not welcome to his wedding unless I dropped the charges against Father. I could not believe that he would send an invitation, yet be so cruel. It was so painful to miss his wedding. I had never missed a family holiday or celebration. Those moments had always been overly important to me, and to miss his wedding was heartbreaking. Soon after, he emailed me the pictures of the day so I could see what I had missed. I would have never imagined that he could be so vindictive.

By this time, I had lost my entire family: my parents, brothers, grandparents, aunts, uncles, and cousins from both sides. This was a loss that cut deeply into who I was. My roots were homespun and engrained with family. Now I had lost them all. I recalled envisioning my brothers getting married, even imagining my children as flower girls and ring bearers. It was all gone.

I slowly came to understand that I never really had family. I had only the illusion of a wonderful family that Mother had made and everyone conformed to. But all along, I was being molded into their lie and I never fit. I had always been told that I talked too much, didn't dress right, didn't wear enough makeup or jewelry, was too fat, lazy and so forth. I came to realize in high school that my parents had an ever–moving bar of accomplishment, with an ever–wavering sense of conditional love; the condition being that I would make them look good.

The day I confronted my parents with the truth was the day that I left the illusion behind. The fairytale had disintegrated into dust. I knew that in missing the wedding, both Mother and Father would be forced to face their families with unanswered questions. The silence spoke volumes. It shattered the image of perfection they had painted all these years, and they would never get it back. Neither would I.

Psalm 27:10

When my father and my mother
forsake me, then the Lord will take me up.
(KJV)

Song

"Not Right Now"
Jason Gray (Gray, 2014)

My Body Speaks

I was in an exam room in a doctor's office. There stood only a few hooded, faceless people with me. I was in my eyes, and my head was invisibly shaking a terrified "no."A hand came from behind and covered my mouth and nose. My eyesight started going into a tunnel as my lungs screamed to breathe. The hand came off my nose and mouth, and my body began to shake violently. Suddenly, I was on the ceiling looking down at my body. I watched what was happening to me and really didn't care. I felt light and peaceful. Suddenly, I recognized Father's arm. His watch was no longer hidden by the robe. He and several more people began to shout, "Lisa! Lisa! Lisa!"

I still didn't care what was happening. I watched them put me on the exam table. My body seemed to be having a seizure. I saw a robed figure walk up with a shot. He put the needle in my arm and immediately I went back into my body. My body felt extremely heavy. I still heard the shouting of my name, but then, I heard nothing at all.

For as long as I could remember, every time I would go to sleep at night, I would hear my name screamed by many voices. The moment I had this memory, the screaming voices stopped. I would hear them no more.

~*~

Several months had passed and Detective McGowen called and asked us to come and talk to the district attorney. Once again, I was terrified, having no idea what to expect. We packed up the kids and went to Minnesota again.

The D.A. was very kind and listened to me carefully. Detective McGowen intended for her to see that I was believable and strong enough for the rigors of trial. She assured me that she would do all she could for me.

When we got back home from the meeting with the D.A., we found out that we were pregnant with our fourth child. I wasn't sure that I could handle the pregnancy along with everything else, but God always knows what He is doing and made a way for me to carry this child. The flashbacks quit and I was able to focus on the family again. It felt so good to have a break.

My body always had difficulty having babies. Stephanie was born four weeks early and Daniel was early by five weeks. The doctors had no explanation for the early births. We almost lost our third baby, Anna, at twenty-four weeks' gestation. My contractions were three minutes apart and we had doctors, nurses, and neonatologists running in and out of the room trying to stop the contractions. The neonatologist told us that Anna was coming and there was nothing he could do. He was sorry, but it was too early and the baby would not survive.

James prayed with me over our baby. Sue called all around getting many wonderful people praying for us and a miracle happened. I stopped dilating and the contractions slowed down. I spent the next three months on total bed rest. James' mother took our children to stay with them, while he and I spent the next three months making trips back and forth to the emergency room. My doctor was amazing and did a lot to keep the baby from coming early. Our little Anna was born almost full term.

Now four years later I was pregnant again. We started praying immediately, and prayer warriors joined us. I tried to take it as easy as I could, but with three other children – Stephanie now eight, Daniel now six, and Anna now four, the demands of motherhood did not slow down.

I started pre-term labor on 9/11 after the stress of watching the towers fall and listening to the news all day. I was eighteen weeks along and the doctors were able to control the contractions with pills that calmed my system down, but after a couple months the pills no longer stopped the contractions. We went through the same thing at the hospital that we had gone through with our Anna, but this time, we were at twenty-two weeks gestation.

I was back on bed rest with the advantage that I could rest on the couch and supervise the kids and home-school them from there. I gained a lot of water weight within a week and towards the end of my pregnancy I had toxemia, which had elevated my blood pressure. The doctor induced and our lovely Cleo was born a few hours later.

The birth of the baby is usually what allows the blood pressure to stabilize, yet my blood pressure did not. I was put back on bed rest. After two long weeks, my blood pressure finally returned to normal.

My unusual pregnancies were another piece of my puzzle. It did not make sense that my body fought taking a baby to term. Now that we knew about the SRA, it made perfect sense. My body remembered the abuse and responded as a survivor. I am so grateful to God for keeping my babies in the womb until they were ready to be born.

After Cleo was born, life once again became very busy. James took a new job in New York and we moved when our little one was six months old. This life change provided another wonderful escape from SRA recovery and I was very grateful for the break. It seemed that any major change in our lives calmed down the flashbacks and gave me a reprieve.

Life went by fast. I was again schooling Stephanie and Daniel, along with a preschooler and crawling baby. We became connected to a new church and our new life had started once again. The nightmares came less and less and I was very hopeful that I had moved through the worst of my past and was near recovery from the SRA trauma. This reprieve however, turned out to be the calm before the storm…

Deuteronomy 28: 11

And the LORD will make you abound in prosperity, in the fruit of your womb and in the fruit of your livestock and in the fruit of your ground, within the land that the LORD swore to your fathers to give you. (English Standard Version)

Song

"The Hurt & The Healer"
Mercy Me (Millard, 2012)

The Letter

I stood in a large clearing in the center of a forest, deep in the middle of nowhere. The clear night had stars overhead and a huge bonfire with a faceless priest in front of it. I stood near the edge of the robed group and no one seemed to be watching me. Slowly, I moved backwards one step at a time. When I reached the edge of the forest, I turned and ran down the only path I could find. I ran fast as I could. (It was dark and I was not able to see the branches and path very well.) My lungs screamed and my heart raced. With a thud, I came to a complete stop. I had run into something large that grabbed a hold of me and was dragged back down the path and taken up front to the priest. I could hear the smirk on his face as he told me that I would never escape. But he was wrong. I could escape into my brain, and so I did.

A few years into my recovery process, my brothers were married and having children of their own. I had not met their wives and I had no way of knowing if their wives had been told the truth of what had happened to me. I was very worried that my nieces and nephews would be abused by Father. There had to be a way to stop Father from sexually abusing his grandchildren and continuing with his Satanic Ritual Abuse. Perpetrators do not stop victimizing and I knew that Father did not want help. I could not fathom my nieces and nephews coming to me in twenty years demanding to know why I had not tried to protect them. There was no way to stay silent and passively allow them to endure Satanic Ritual Abuse. I reasoned that they were very young and could not defend themselves, but maybe I could.

I prayed and asked God what I could do. The answer swelled up inside of me so strongly that I knew I had to do it quickly. Letter writing was the answer. I wanted to tell the wives about the abuse so that they would never leave their children alone with my parents. I wasn't going to try to keep them from having a relationship with my parents. I just wanted them to be watchful and careful whenever my parents were around their children.

The inherent problem with letter writing was that I could not guarantee my sisters-in-law would even get the letters. There was a real possibility that my brothers would intercept the letters and not allow their wives to see them. I spent many days trying to figure out how to get each letter into the moms' hands.

A very good friend of mine was a teacher that I had had in high school. She was a lot of fun and often made me laugh, which was a breath of fresh air in the midst of my struggles. We brainstormed ideas on how I could make sure the letters would be read by my sisters-in-law. We decided that the best way of making sure the letter was received would be to send a second copy of the letter to the mothers-in-law. I would include an explanation as to why I was sending a second copy to them – ensuring their daughters read the letters I had sent them. At the very least, I assumed that there would be a conversation between my brothers and their wives. That was the best I could hope for.

Writing the letter proved to be challenging. I felt the need to include some of the proof I had collected. There was no way to explain the last few years. How could I tell them about the nightmares, flashbacks, panic attacks, and how the pieces of my life had finally come together? If they did not know of SRA or believe in the reality of the practice, I knew they would not listen. After weeks of praying and anguishing and not sleeping, I finally came up with the wording.

I told my sisters-in-law why I had sent them the letter and that I had also sent copies to their mothers. I strongly stated my sole purpose was to protect their children. I told them my story and the great danger their children were in. I warned them to never leave their children alone with my parents. I assured them that I was not looking to break their relationship with my parents, but that I wanted them to be aware in order to keep their children safe. After the letter was sent, I felt a huge weight lift off my shoulders. I prayed they would receive my letter and truly think my advice through.

~*~

A few months later there was a knock on my door. A mailman handed me a manila envelope that I had to sign for. It was from one of my brothers. When we had moved to New York, I had attempted to keep our address and phone number unlisted, which made me feel safer. In a phone call I had a few weeks later with him, he told me he had sent it registered mail to show me how stupid I was to think I could stay hidden. I took his call as a threat and lost my feeling of safety.

The envelope contained a very long manuscript with a huge list of the reasons why I was a liar. The manuscript claimed I was trying to ruin the relationships between my parents and their wives. My brother declared that Father was a "great man." He had scrounged up all sorts of lies and distortions and sent copies of the document he had written to all of my close friends, family, pastors, and college friends. I was horrified!

I sobbed for hours and waited for James to come home from work so I could show the document to him. I couldn't get past the cruelty of what my brother had done. In his attempt to try to make Father look like the good guy, he worked hard to make me look like an idiot to all the people in my life. Most of the recipients of the document had no idea about Father and my abusive past. I hadn't shared it with them. The limited sense of privacy that I had left was now gone.

James suggested calling my best friend from college and getting her take on it, but to give it a couple days' rest first. It sounded like a good strategy. When I called my friend, she told me that she and her husband had received the document, and when they realized what it was they threw it away without reading it. She knew some of our other friends had done the same thing. She assured me that the people who knew me also knew my sense of integrity, and that no matter what the letter said, they would not believe it to be true. She certainly showed me why she was my best friend.

Psalm 27: 12

Deliver me not over unto the will of mine enemies: for false witnesses are risen up against me, and such as breathe out cruelty. (KJV)

Song

"The Warrior is a Child"
Twila Paris (Paris, 1984)

I'll Try Anything

~*~

I stood before a man who was tied down on the table of sacrifice. I was in the middle of the circle of the faceless bodies in their black robes and hoods. Chanting wafted through the candle smoke, saying, "Do it. Do it. Do it." Over and over again it rang through the air.

I looked down and saw a huge knife in my hand. I realized that I would be the one who would make the sacrifice this time. My eyes were huge with terror as my head shook imperceptibly back and forth in a small plea of "no." Hands came from behind and wrapped around my hands holding the knife. The knife rose high up in the air and paused over the sacrifice. Then my hands were forced downward as the knife pierced through the body.

"Guilty, guilty, guilty," wafted the chants on the smoke.

Again, my head vibrated back and forth "no." It took a few minutes for me to realize that I hadn't killed him. When I looked down, I saw that his head was missing. He was already dead.

~*~

The reprieve from nightmares and flashbacks lasted a few years with Cleo's birth and our move to New York. When they returned, they came back with a vengeance. Once again, I went into counseling and had to retell the trauma of my childhood.

The symptoms of PTSD (post-traumatic stress disorder) were really bad. I was triggered a lot. A "trigger" is when something I would see would pull me emotionally back into a ritual. For me, mice always threw me into a full-blown panic attack. If I felt verbally attacked or was the object of someone's anger, it would trigger a memory of a ritual.

One day a mouse ran across my kitchen floor. I was screaming and crying. James picked me up and carried me to our bedroom and there I stayed until he caught the mouse. There were so many triggers that we could not predict what they would be. I was becoming less functional again. Homeschooling became the focus because no matter what was happening, my children needed to be educated. My ever-faithful James was once again taking over chores around the house and trying to keep me going.

I can never be thankful enough for my new counselor, Meredith. She kept going into the trenches of SRA with me. She had never worked with an SRA survivor before, but she had an associate who had and she helped Meredith to help me. There was a technique called EMDR (Eye Movement and Desensitization and Reprocessing) and she wanted me to try it.

The idea behind this therapy is that traumatic events are captured in the back of one's brain. Processing of the traumatic memories takes place in the front of the brain. Talking through the trauma helps to process the event to help the victim to have a lesser emotional response to trauma, but it takes a very long time. EMDR speeds this process up. This therapy is accomplished through eye movement. By stimulating one side of the brain and then the other, a person is able to process the trauma much more quickly than through regular talk therapy.

I held a sensor in each hand; one buzzing and then the other, back and forth. Meredith would talk about us being on a train and driving by the rituals and just watching, not actually being in them. I had trouble with the train because I could not stay on it. I would get right into the middle of the ritual, once again becoming the little girl suffering abuse. The idea was to keep going through the memory, over and over, until it no longer held power over you. It sounded strange, but I was desperate. I needed help.

Meredith and I worked hard with EMDR. We went through each SRA memory that I had, one by one. It was awful and painful, but it took the sting out of the trauma left over from the ritual. I would cry hysterically with the emotional pain overwhelming me and felt like my chest was going to explode. Meredith kept her voice calm and added a 'theophostic' element to it by asking me where Jesus was in the situation. I would look at it with new eyes and imagine Jesus "fixing it" by rescuing me and getting me out of the experience. I saw Jesus being angry with the perpetrators for doing such things to me. It was very healing.

I felt EMDR really had merit as I connected it to a situation with Daniel from 9/11. On that day, my husband called to tell me that an airplane had crashed into one of the Twin Towers in New York City. I turned the news on minutes before the second airplane hit the second tower. Daniel was six at the time and was mesmerized by the shock of what was happening. For the next few weeks, he worked his way through his trauma, all on his own.

He would build two towers out of his blocks, fly an airplane towards it, yell, "Oh, no!" and then crash the plane into the building, knocking down all the blocks. He repeated this over and over and over, until I finally called Sue and told her that if he did it one more time, I was going to scream. She explained to me that he was working it out and that I had to let him do it at his own pace.

The changes came slowly. He began crashing the plane onto the floor before it hit the building. He would look at the plane mournfully for all the people that died. Then he would do it again. Eventually, he had the bad guys taken off of the plane by the police before the airplane left the ground.

My son, at such a tender age, was doing his own EMDR therapy. He kept going over and over the trauma until he could understand it and then he fixed it to save the lives of all the people. What my son was able to do was what Meredith was teaching me.

Each ritual was a struggle to process. None of them were easy to visit, and they were all…almost impossible to speak of. They were certainly not something I wanted to go back to and examine.

My philosophy of recovery was pushing through so I could get past it, and that is what Meredith and I did.

One day, we tackled a particularly difficult ritual. There was killing involved and I just could not handle it. I was back in my eyes, doing the almost imperceptible shaking "no" of my head. I was not aware of the "present" at all. I think I scared Meredith, for she tried everything she could think of to pull me back into the present. "Feel the couch, see the room, calm your breathing," and whatever she could think of. I was screaming in terror and sobbing uncontrollably.

Meredith really struggled with the specifics of the horrible things that had happened to me in that abusive memory and had to go into counseling herself to help her cope with me. I found out that she had suffered secondary trauma, which occurred while reliving the trauma with me, yet she never pulled back or asked for a break. She bravely kept me going week after week until we had gone through each ritual.

EMDR was an amazing therapeutic tool and really helped me with the extreme terror that I was unable to respond to during the rituals as a child. I was now able to look back at the rituals without being an emotional wreck for days. I became more functional for my family again, which was an incredible relief for us all.

Isaiah 63: 18-19

Remember ye not the former things, neither consider the things of old. Behold, I will do a new thing; now it shall spring forth; shall ye not know it? I will even make a way in the wilderness, and rivers in the desert. (KJV)

Song

"God Will Make A Way"
Don Moen (Moen, 2003)

Custody Battle

I was lying on the floor in a white gown, unable to move, although I was not tied. The room was dark, with candles, smoke, and chanting. The circle around me was filled with people in grim reaper-like robes and face concealing hoods. Inside the circle, some people were dancing, one woman was completely naked. I watched knowing something bad would happen to me because I was in the white gown. The woman came over and started dancing around me. She then stepped over my head and urinated on my face. Even though I was just my eyes, they burned.

~*~

I received a phone call from my brother's wife almost a year after I had written the letter to my sisters-in-law and their mothers. Eileen told me that after she got my letter, she was livid because my brother had never told her what had happened to me. I had been correct in my fears: no one had told Eileen why I did not associate with my family. She had taken their baby and left, and my brother was suing her for a legal separation, along with full custody of their child. The reason he gave was that his wife "was crazy because she believed his crazy sister." I was stunned. I explained to her that I never intended to break up their marriage; I only wanted her to be able to watch out for her child.

Eileen called often to talk about her life with my brother, the lawsuit, and how he was financially hurting her. Some of her stories seemed to change from time to time, which never made sense. But I told her I would do anything I could to help, the safety of her son being my utmost concern.

A court date was set for the end of December for custody of their child and I was to testify. That meant a long, icy, winter drive to stay with James's parents, since they were closer to court and could watch our four children. We arrived on the court date to hear a judge say they were postponing the hearing until the second week in January. This meant we were stuck in Illinois until the next trial date.

While we waited for the court date, I received a call from Detective McGowen asking me to write up some episodes of Father raping me at home. He also told me that the Sheriff was starting a media blitz for my case, without naming names of course. They asked for other SRA survivors from the 70's to call in to help with my case.

After the ad aired, I received a phone call from my teacher friend. She told me of the media blitz and that it had caused quite a bit of interest in the community. She informed me that the reporters were scrambling to try to find out who the victim was. Just the thought of any of them finding me made me ill.

Detective McGowen came up with two real leads. The first one was a woman who talked to him but was too afraid to come forward in a court case. This was a major problem in our case because often SRA victims are terrified of being killed if they ever tell what happened to them. He was also called into the jail to talk with an inmate who claimed SRA had happened to him. Detective McGowen said that if he had put what happened to me side by side to what had happened to him, it would have been like hearing the same story. Unfortunately, he was incarcerated, which the defense would use against his credibility.

This was the first time I had "real" outside validation on the SRA. I really did not need it anymore. I knew enough that I could never doubt it happened to me. The Detective said that we would need to have more than one survivor standing up with me in court; there would have to be at least three of us. He went back to the woman but she again refused. He explained to me that the jury would struggle to believe that SRA exists, especially in rural Minnesota. It would be an uphill battle and the D.A. didn't think she could win the case without getting a third survivor on the stand. Detective McGowen also told me that if I had only filed for the sexual abuse by my father, they would have gone to court long ago and most likely I would have won.

In January, James and I once again travelled to court for Eileen's custody hearing. This time the hearing was put off until March. I couldn't believe it. I told Eileen's attorney that we didn't live in the area, the expense of the travel was huge for us, and that my husband was a professor and would be working. It didn't seem to matter to Eileen's lawyer one bit.

In March, James had to take a couple days off work so we could go to the hearing. Again we packed our children in the van and made the long trip to James' parents' house. This time Detective McGowen was with us. He was there to share the investigation details with them that he legally could. Pastor Molnar, my childhood pastor, was also at the hearing. He would be able to share conversations with my parents that did not fall under the pastor/parishioner privilege. Only the conversations that occurred in the formality of the pastor's office were protected legally.

My brother's representation included my parents, my brothers and their wives, aunts and uncles, and Pastor Baker, who was my parents' pastor. James and I had talked to Pastor Baker twice when we were having the meeting with my parents. Pastor Baker even removed my parents from serving in the children's ministry. I was surprised that he was now on their side.

It seemed that I was in the center of the whole custody hearing. Eileen did not want my brother alone with their baby because she was afraid he would have my parents babysit. The abuse that had happened to me was the reason Eileen had left my brother.

I was called in for four grueling hours of questions on the witness stand. It was very odd. My brother's lawyer laid into me something fierce and tried to make me look like an idiot. Eileen's lawyer never objected to any of the ill treatment I was given. The judge was starting to lecture her attorney about not objecting when he should, and a few times the judge objected for him.

Her lawyer had told me before the custody battle started to answer all questions yes or no, and that he would redirect when it was his turn. He didn't. He just sat there the entire time looking like he had no idea what was going on. There was a window at the door of the courtroom that one could see through when on the stand. During my testimony, Father kept walking by and staring at me. I got his message loud and clear. The lawyers finally finished and I walked out in an exhausted daze.

James was taken in and his testimony was finished quickly. Once again, Eileen's attorney seemed spacey and never redirected questions to James so he could clarify the yes or no answers he had given. James came out feeling like he had let me down.

Pastor Molnar was in and out in five minutes with a strange expression on his face. My brother's lawyer shut him down immediately for pastor privilege, and Pastor Molnar was not allowed to explain why that rule did not apply in this circumstance. He was not allowed to give any testimony at all in the courtroom.

Detective McGowen was sent in and came out in the same manner. He was told he couldn't speak because it was an ongoing investigation. The detective told us that that was not true, but he hadn't been allowed to tell the court.

Another peculiarity was that no one was allowed in the courtroom to observe. No one. Without knowing what was going on, there was no reason to stay, so we left. Eileen never bothered to call to tell me the outcome of the hearing.

I called Eileen the next day to find out the verdict and she was surprisingly angry with me. She said she had decided to go back to live with my brother, their separation being over. I was happy they were getting back together; I never wanted them to be separated in the first place.

Since that hearing, Eileen and I have had only a few conversations. At first, we tried to keep in touch, but my emotions were on edge with every phone call and I was triggered for a few days after that. I realized that I was putting James and the kids through too much and I had the power to stop this. So, the next time she called, I told her I couldn't talk anymore. She said, "Well, at least we got to the truth."

I had heard that sentence long before, from my brother. It gave me a chill. I felt saddened and disheartened. It got me thinking about how Eileen's lawyer had told James and me to answer my brother's lawyer's questions with a "yes" or "no" and he would redirect, yet never redirected. His passivity in the courtroom had been called into question by even the judge. It gave me questions about the whole separation scenario.

Eileen invited James, our children, and me to visit her and her baby before the whole court case had come up. The first time we had met her she strongly insisted we go to the house that she and my brother had lived in together, and where my brother was still living. She showed us how there was no furniture in the baby's room, although the indentations in the carpet looked like everything had been moved far more recently than what she indicated. There was also the time that my aunt (the only aunt that staunchly stood beside me, called me, and sent Christmas presents every year) found my brother, Eileen, and the baby together at the mall when they were supposed to be in the midst of the challenging part of their separation. Knowing my aunt communicated with us, my sister-in-law called to explain to me that they were just trying to get things worked out, although she had informed us that they were so mad at each other, they could barely talk. Something just did not fit. I was relieved to get my brother and Eileen's problems out of our home.

Proverbs 12: 19, 20, 22

The lip of truth shall be established for ever: but a lying tongue is but for a moment. Deceit is in the heart of them that imagine evil: but to the counselors of peace is joy. Lying lips are an abomination to the Lord: but they that deal truly are his delight. (KJV)

Song

"Good Good Father"
Chris Tomlin (Barrett & Brown, 2015)

Promise Lost

I'm not the mom I thought I'd be
As close I held my first baby

Looking at her future bright
Thinking I could do it right

I'd keep her fed, safe and warm
Always gentle would be the norm

Soon there were two, then three and four
My wondrous kids I did adore

But something niggled in my brain
Some kind of danger I couldn't name

Did I need to keep it out?
Or look to see what threat was about?

I had to search against my will
To check it out, see if was real

Terror climbed, upon my back
It was either me, or kids attacked

I did not know, how to fight
So I cried both day and night

My kids looked on, sadly at me
Wondering where went their promised mommy

I thought it might, ease in time
Heal my past, regain my mind

The house got dirty, the laundry towered
I couldn't cook, my mood it glowered

Their mommy often, sick in bed
They took care of me instead

I wasn't always, patient kind
I hurt their feelings, oh time rewind

I stand here now, looking back
Over years I can't retract

House still dirty, dishes piled
Laundry toppling, housework a trial

Keeping them safe, won out in the end
They weren't abused, not now – not then

I see the years, have made them tough
So maybe I did, just enough…

Finding Survivors

~*~

I sat in the church pew and stared out the window at the huge flakes coming down one after the other. It looked like a big snow globe scene. My pastor's wife, Elizabeth, came over and sat in front of me. She knew that I had sexual abuse and SRA in my past and thought a conference they were having about healing abuse would be very helpful. It wasn't.

They mentioned that SRA existed, but they weren't able to cover it in the conference... another dead end for me in my search for help from SRA recovery in the Christian world. At the moment, people were supposed to be going to counselors for prayer, but I just didn't see the point.

"Look at those snowflakes, Elizabeth," I said, "Each one is a memory I have to deal with, and they are piling up. Christians aren't jumping in to help, so who will?"

I could feel her looking at me as I continued staring out the window. She kindly encouraged me to keep going and not give up.

~*~

It was time to stop expecting specific SRA help from the Christian community and look into non-Christian help. I had a strong need to connect with people who were also SRA survivors. Not only had I never met one, I also had never had a counselor who had counseled anyone with SRA. I finally googled some groups on the internet, and prayed about which one to join.

Joining a group was a huge step for me. There was always that fear of the cult finding out that I was talking and making good on their promise to kill me. Out of desperation, I joined anyway. I felt that God led me to one, and I made some really good friends. Everyone would write about what they had gone through, how they were feeling, and others would jump in and write about encouragement, advice or their experience. It still amazes me how closely related their stories were to mine. I wished I hadn't waited thirteen years to find them.

As I started getting to know the other survivors, I realized that the majority believed in God because they had seen the demonic in action. The elements of Christianity that were used in their abuse, however, became the very things they stayed away from as adults, including Bibles, communion, crosses, and any talk of the blood of Christ. Men in authority, such as pastors, God the Father, and Jesus their brother, were also avoided. Very few were able to go to church, for church was an extremely difficult place to be.

My heart ached for the courageous men and women who were survivors. Their lives were very broken like mine. The SRA survivors in my group demonstrated a huge range of how they were able to live their lives. Many were on emotional or physical disability. Some were not functional at all. Some were able to pull themselves together for work, but were a wreck the rest of the time. I realized I was blessed to be doing as well as I was. A great number of survivors were homeless or institutionalized, into drugs or used alcohol to dim the pain. They were alone in a world where people couldn't begin to understand what they had been through or how to help them.

The first SRA survivor I had contact with was Denise. She was very good at articulating her emotions and experience. She had no contact with her abusive family and was alone in the world, but content with her dogs, cats, fish, and therapist. She had found her safety in animals that poured their love back into her. After months and months of talking online, we decided to try talking over the phone. We were both terrified, for our trust in each other had to be huge for this step. Once we started talking, there was no going back. We shared our lives, our struggles, successes and brokenness with each other.

Denise is an extremely courageous survivor. She was able to make a complete break from her family of abuse and work toward healing with great strength. She has been able to hold down a good paying job in the midst of many emotional and physical scars. She was a gift from God.

It was from Denise that I was finally able to piece together the SRA elements of my life and put them in context. I found out what books had helped her and bought them to read, hoping they give me more healing insight. I never had to be strong with Denise. I could just be me with no mask hiding my emotions. She listened and somehow understood whatever I was going through.

Denise had a therapist who knew about SRA. I didn't really know they existed. I had had five therapists to date, and I was the first SRA survivor each one had worked with. I had prayed that someday, I would find a Christian therapist who had experience with survivors.

Denise and I talked over the phone for years and decided we should meet in person. Again, the trust in this was huge, but I couldn't wait to meet this amazing woman. My family went on vacation near where she lived, and she joined me for breakfast. I hugged her tightly with emotions overwhelming me. Because of Denise, I was not alone in my journey any longer. She was an important element in my healing.

When Denise was suffering emotionally and needed a counselor to help her through it, she called Dr. Jefferson. Even though she had gotten the therapist's name from the phone book, Dr. Jefferson saw Denise right away. When Denise told her about the SRA and how other therapists had refused to work with her because of the satanic element of the abuse, Dr. Jefferson did not flinch. Not only did she take her on, but she studied SRA and joined groups with other therapists to learn about how to specifically help Denise with her recovery. I find this professionalism amazing.

Brianna was the next friend I met and she was not doing well. She had been very sick and feared that she was going to die. Brianna couldn't stand to be inside buildings as she would have extreme panic attacks. Her husband moved her to Hawaii so that they could live on the beach. The idea was that she could live outside, even when it was rainy and cool. She would spend her days standing in the ocean hoping the salt would take away the immense pain she always suffered.

We talked periodically and my heart was filled with compassion for what she had endured. Brianna lived in a constant state of being triggered. The only bits of peace she got were when we talked about God and prayed together. I was told that Brianna ended up dying on that beach. My heart breaks for Brianna and so many others like her.

Grace is from Canada and has become a very sweet addition to my friends. She works hard to keep herself afloat financially, even when she was having a particularly hard time emotionally. Her story is different, in that it wasn't her parents who had taken her to the SRA cult. Unfortunately, her family has refused to believe or help her. Eventually, they cut her out of their lives. Grace and I keep contact through the internet and I consider her one of my best friends. I always enjoy the talks we have. Grace is another courageous survivor who amazes me with her ability to keep going. I would love to meet her someday!

I also met a friend from Australia. Benjamin was abused by his parents and is on disability, due to the SRA. He lives his life taking trips with his camera and taking amazing pictures of great beauty. We don't talk often, but it is always fun to catch up with him and his adventurous life.

Through processing with my friends, I was able to piece together more of my life. When I was young, I always doodled a star with a circle around it. Never just a star, always with the circle.

As an adult, I found myself doodling the star and circle one day and realized it was a pentagram!

~*~

My body continued to send me signals. Autumn was always the time of year when I seemed to fall apart. It wasn't just Halloween, although death, blood, the grim reaper, masks, cats, witches, and so on were something I had already pieced together. I learned that death is a part of the rituals of the fall season, and it has helped to explain my emotional issues that reoccur that time of the year.

Another mystery solved was my attempts to go to our church for its Wednesday night prayer meeting. I love to pray and I love church, so it seemed the natural thing to do. Unfortunately, I always left feeling sad and with the feeling that something was wrong, so I would quit going. After a few months, I wondered why I didn't go to mid-week prayer, and I would try it again. Still, I ended with the same results. I realized from talking with my group of friends that I was being triggered by the chairs at the prayer meeting. The chairs were always set up in a circle and that made sense. Circle settings in a church sanctuary are not good for SRA survivors.

~*~

Discussions with SRA friends helped me make sense of my wedding day. My wedding day had me shaking like a leaf as I walked down the aisle. So much so that James and the pastor looked at me with shock and asked if I was okay. Through the group, I learned that being the center of any kind of attention can be a big trigger. I recognized why I hated having birthday parties that focused on me, being the center of attention sent my body into crazy panic mode.

My hyper vigilance around men was also explained. Whenever I am around men, I am always checking out their eyes. From their eyes, I gathered information as to whether they are in a good mood or not, if there is evil there, and whether I feel safe to be around them. I knew Father's eyes always narrowed at me when he got angry and was going to rape me. I found this same eye-checking hyper vigilance was also common in other SRA survivors.

The list of revelations goes on and on. At this point in my healing journey, I was no longer fighting myself or telling my body to stop over-reacting. The knowledge that I reacted like other survivors helped me to accept the SRA scars in my life.

During this time, I finally found a book specifically for SRA survivors. It was just what I needed. Safe Passage to Healing, by Chrystine Oksana became a godsend with an amazing amount of research and answers.

The book taught about programming in the cult. In my life, I learned there was no way to escape. This was solidified when I tried to run away and ran into a sentry. The graveyard scene was to teach me to never tell, and to understand that if I did, I would die.

"There are many similarities between victims of ritual abuse and prisoners of war (POWs) subjected to rigorous thought reform. As with some of these prisoners, ritual abuse survivors are primarily indoctrinated through the three T's: torture, terror, and threats. The difference is that these victims are not trained soldiers, but usually young children. The war zone is not a foreign country but the child's home, school, or another "safe" environment. The tormentors are not a recognized "enemy." They are the child's primary caregivers. There is no escape and no end to the war." (Oksana, 2001)

This passage succinctly describes my experience. I also learned through Osama's book that SRA survivors have a "handler." The handler is cult appointed to keep the survivor in line, keeping the mind control strong, and not allowing the survivor to tell about the abuse. This handling goes on even if the victim leaves the cult as an adult.

When I read this, I realized that Mother was my handler: Father never tried to get me back in check, it was always my mother. This explained the constant phone calls where my mother tried to talk me out of thinking or dealing with the past or even getting a counselor. Mother kept asking me if I was going to a counselor and telling me not to trust them. Mother's behavior finally made sense when I began to understand how a cult family was structured.

It's amazing how many answers started coming at this point. It truly opened my eyes to how incredibly wicked ritual abuse is, not only to the child, but to the adult the child grows into as well. The information helped me to make sense out of the cult. I was an adult now, but there was a little Lisa somewhere deep inside that was still terrified and thinking the abuse was still going on. To get healing, I would have to find the young Lisa still inside me. I would have to help her to heal, or I wouldn't.

Proverbs 27:17

*Iron sharpeneth iron; so a man
sharpeneth the countenance of his friend.
(KJV)*

Song

I Will Be Your Friend
Amy Grant (Deviller, Hosier, & Lewis, I Will Be
Your Friend, 1997)

A Note from Denise

~*~

I am Lisa's dear friend Denise, and we have been friends for seven years. We met online at a support group for SRA survivors. When we started talking, we realized how similar our abuse was at the hands of our "families". It's very difficult for survivors to get and maintain friendships with other survivors, but Lisa and I have stayed friends and have even been able to meet twice and share a meal. I've seen my friend Lisa grow over the years a great deal.

It's very brave of Lisa to write this book and get her story out there. When I first read Lisa's book, I couldn't put it down because I related to it so much personally. Recovering from SRA is a very long, lifelong journey. I don't think anyone ever completely heals from these horrible crimes. Lisa is very brave to have been able to marry and have a family of her own. Many survivors get in very unhealthy, abusive relationships because of their past, but Lisa has a very healthy and happy life with her family. Unfortunately, I was not able to get married and have children of my own. It has such an impact on a survivor's life.

I've always been close to God, but Lisa's faith has helped me to grow even closer in my relationship with Him. I think society needs to know about these horrific crimes and step up to try to stop it. By writing a book such as Lisa has, the word will get out there even more.

I highly recommend this book to survivors and non survivors alike. It would educate non-survivors about SRA and show them that SRA is a heinous crime and really exists. For the survivor, it will validate his or her experience and him or her to know that they are not alone.

Denise
A Survivor

I Saw You

I saw you the other day
Just a flash
A shock out of the darkness
A glimpse of the girl
I wanted to forget

I had seen your shadow
Stopping by
Over the years
But I pushed you away
To stay the tears

But in that flash
That moment suspended through time
That raw spot in my chest
Reached out to you
To understand

I did not want
To meet you again
You disrupted my life
Time after time
Even as you were forgotten

That touch
Brief as it was
Opened the vault
I had sealed for eternity
Long ago

You sent another flash
And there you were
Bruised dirty alone
Forgotten
I had put you there

I looked long and hard
Your desperation
And I walked up to you
Slapped your face
How dare you

You curl in a ball
I stomp away
My chest bleeds
My head pounds
I hear your cry

I can't sleep
The echo of your cry
The pitiful picture
You display
Takes my appetite away

What is wrong with you
Leave me alone
Go away
I cannot deal with you today
Or ever

I can't breathe
The pain in my chest
Reaches out to the one
I can no longer leave behind

Another flash
I walk back
To the past
I will not hurt you anymore

You look up at me
Tears of the unwashed
Forgotten child
I look at your face
You are me

All you want
Is for me to pick you up
Accept legitimacy
You are the one
Who never lied to me

I take you back
To the present
The only place
I can keep you safe
Protected

No more fighting
Now you are loved
Believed
Accepted
The only things you wanted
All along
~*~

Here We Go Again

I was angry and pulled the hood off the man who was raping me. He was so enraged that the veins on his forehead were sticking out. He put his hand around my throat, lifting me slightly up so I could not breathe. He told me that if I ever did something like that again he would personally kill me.

In the midst of the court proceedings of my brother's legal separation and child custody case, Detective McGowen had called. He and the Sheriff had contacted the media asking other survivors to come forward. The media was scrambling trying to find the identity of the woman who had filed the charges, and wanted to know what the specific complaint was. I couldn't imagine how my life would change if they figured out who I was. The tip line had received many calls and was sifting through them all.

The stress of my brother's court case and the media blitz made my life feel like it was spinning out of control. The PTSD symptoms were in full force.

A few months after the court case I had a stroke. I was lying down in the bedroom when all of a sudden it felt like someone had slammed the right side of my face toward the left. I couldn't talk and just made garbled sounds and crazy laughter. I couldn't get my body to respond like normal. The next thing I knew, there were men all around working on me. I could only see halfway up their bodies and I saw doubles of everything. The paramedics found my glucose level was low, so they gave me some glycerin, which helped my body get me going back on track. My symptoms were confusing. Some of the paramedics thought it was a stroke and one thought it was low glucose. The paramedics asked me if I wanted to go to the hospital, but I refused. The hospital was the last place I wanted to be because I would have no control over my body. Others would be in control and that terrified me. It took a few days of having to lift my one knee purposefully when I walked, and I had episodes of tipping over, but otherwise I seemed normal. A month later, I went to see my neurologist for a normal migraine checkup. I told her what happened and she ordered an MRI. When the results came back, there was a spot on my brain. I had suffered a stroke.

Life changed after my stroke. I could no longer roller-blade or ice skate because of the problem of tipping over. I couldn't even walk by myself without someone there to help steady me. In one small moment, I lost so much independence.

After a brief reprieve, the flashbacks started again. I would still feel incredible pain for days before the flashback would appear. I still fought against the memory coming out with everything I had, which took a great deal of energy. But the memories always came out in the end. Still, I was hopeful that one day they would just stop. But the flashbacks did not stop and I experienced the worst one to date.

Up until this point, the worst flashback I had was when I was forced to "kill" the already "dead man". This flashback hit me particularly hard. It fragmented my thoughts and emotions, even though I hadn't really killed the man. In my mind, I could see the knife, smoke, candles, and all the people in their hooded robes. It took me a year to deal with this image and to process the terror, feelings, and flashes of what had actually happened. The process was like a cycling DVD that ran over and over again.

This particular memory triggered a sad few years of being unable to go to church. I kept getting triggered at church, having the fight or flight syndrome hit me when I least expected it. I would run out of church to sob uncontrollably while waiting at the car until James caught up with me to take me home. It was humiliating.

People at church meant well when they prayed, they liked to pray that the blood of Jesus would cover me and the situation. Rituals were filled with buckets of blood that were spread all over people, so when they would pray the blood of Jesus, it would intensify the flashback. A candle had also been placed on the cross at the front of the sanctuary, and every time I saw it I saw a circle of people in their robes and hoods covering their faces. Therefore, each time I walked into church, I was immediately triggered. So, I had to start staying home.

James and I talked with our pastor about my need to stay away from church. Our pastor showed great compassion and asked what he could do to help me. I asked him to just give me space. Our pastor was really sweet in doing just that, and it was a long couple of years before I could go back. He finally agreed to take the candle off the cross, which stopped the flashback problem immediately.

A year after the last flashback that threw me so badly, I had an even worse one. This one I cannot talk about. This flashback took me two years to process and to calm down.

My kids had begun to explain to their friends what was going on. If I happened to get triggered when they were with their friends at the house, they calmly explained it. My oldest was at an age to date, and she had a boyfriend. I was terrified that when he heard about what had happened to me, he wouldn't want anything to do with our family. When he visited our home, my emotions were on high alert. If I felt something bothering me, I would disappear into my bedroom. When I did get triggered one day, Stephanie gave her boyfriend a small glimpse into my world and he handled it well. My panic didn't seem to change anything. What a relief! I still worry about how my past and healing process will influence my kids' friendships. I pray for mercy and grace whenever my kids choose to tell them, and wisdom with how much to share.

Psalm 6:6

I am weary with my groaning; all the night make I my bed to swim; I water my couch with my tears.

Song

"Lord Reign in Me"
Brenton Brown (Brown, 2006)
~*~

Please Understand

I look across the ocean
Of this thing called life
I'm sitting in my little boat
The water, cold as ice

I paddle left, I paddle right
Until my muscles' burning
My little boat, it almost sunk
Because the waves were churning

A ship it gaily comes up by
Filled with my friends and fam
They call to me to hurry up
Not happy where I am

"What's wrong with you?" they ask of me
"We are going fast
So hurry up, be on your way
Don't delve in your past"

They're in a ship I'm in a boat
They don't relate to mine
While I silently row and row
They laugh and enjoy their time

Don't they see I can't get out?
I'm stuck here in my little boat
If I could only be with them
And in their ship just float

But I am here and they are there
It's not been by my choosing
Don't tell me I should bail out
As if in life I'm losing

Please understand, I plead with you
My boat will keep on going
With it I will always be
Rowing, rowing, rowing

Don't you see, can you not hear
How my heart is weeping
So please be kind and realize
Different vessels we are keeping

I am tired and all worn out
Day by day I row and row
Don't look at me and shake your head
Why must I go so slow

I look ahead for you and see
You anchored to safe land
I stop and stare and am aware
You'll never understand

The Toll

~*~

All day I had the feeling of choking, like something was caught halfway down my throat. Later in the evening the flashback hit:

I was tied down, naked and spread eagle. The circle of chanting, robed and hooded people surrounded me. I was near an altar. A demonic, terrifying voice said, "I am Michael. I am pleased. Go ahead and do as I have directed you to do. Remember to love everyone – everyone in this room. Don't leave anyone out. Then and only then will you have peace. But leave your offering for me." The man got on top of me and forced himself down my throat. It was down too far so I couldn't breathe and I was choking. He said, "You are mine and you will always be mine." As he pulled out of my mouth, I vomited. He slapped me across the face. Vomiting was not allowed.

The flashback explained the throat problem I had experienced all day. It certainly fit. I was left exhausted and terrified.

~*~

As I am writing this book, I am coming off of a year of multiple panic attacks. I was even contemplating suicide at one point. I was having several panic attacks a week, and I even had one in front of a beloved uncle on James's side of the family, which was downright humiliating. I needed help, and I found two therapists who jumped into my emotional pit and made a major difference in my life.

Health wise, I was at my worst. Physically during the past few years I had had intractable migraines, severe breathing issues, asthma, a walled over sinus, short ischemic sight loss in each eye, loss of some peripheral vision, and cyclical vomiting syndrome. All of these current physical ailments, along with the pregnancy problems, could be traced back to the childhood abuse.

The sinus issue was due to a closed sinus cavity. There was no opening to allow drainage. The doctor said that the condition could be caused by previous surgery or past trauma. With all the times the abusers held their hands over my mouth and nose so I couldn't breathe, this condition made perfect sense. So, I had surgery. The doctor literally drilled a hole inside my nose into the cavity.

I was also having coughing spasms so severe that I could not catch my breath. There were ambulance runs and several emergency visits for this condition. The doctors found that the right middle lobe of my lung was scarred at the main bronchus. This was trapping air that needed to be exhaled. Again, this, along with the asthma, could be caused by previous surgery or past trauma.

I asked the surgeon about the possibility of it being from having my air supplies cut off so many times, and he told me "absolutely." Taking out the lobe was the only option, and it was a painful one.

I still had a chronic cough that went into spasms, even after the lung surgery. I was finally sent to an ear, nose and throat specialist. An ultrasound taken of my vocal chords, found that there was some damage. They were not symmetrical and had what they termed "vocal cord dysfunction." Again, I asked the doctor if this could go back to the abuse. She thought it was very likely.

Cyclical Vomiting Syndrome (CVS) is a horrible disease. I would start vomiting, with diarrhea, and have extreme pain in my abdomen which caused me to roll around the bathroom floor in agony. A CVS episode could last for one to seven hours. Intestinal issues are very common for abuse survivors.

The book "The Body Keeps the Score" by Bessel Van Der Kolk, is an interesting read, which explains how the body responds to abuse, even when the person has not yet recalled that they were abused. The majority of the health issues that I have had led right back to the abuse.

While I was at my worst physically, I was on an emotional roller coaster. For the first time, I started taking antidepressants and anti-anxiety meds. The decision to take the medication was hard for me because I know God heals, and know many Christians believe that taking medication is contrary to their faith in God. However, I realized that Christians take blood pressure meds, wear glasses, get casts on their arms or legs, and go to doctors. I prayed about the decision and had peace.

I also started going to a psychiatrist. She put me on meds to calm my body down. The assumption the doctors were making was that my body was going into fight or flight mode all the time, and that I had to find ways to calm it down. I went into breathing therapy to learn how to relax my body as well as open my vocal cords to stop the coughing.

I had a lot of anxiety, panic attacks, migraines, lung damage, and abdominal migraines. I was very discouraged and my doctors were trying a variety of strategies to help me. One doctor sent me to a gastro-intestinal (gi) therapist, something I had never heard of before. Dr. Ann was the lifeline I needed (as I was at a suicidal low). She taught me much in so many practical ways.

Dr. Ann taught me to breathe and relax. She had me set up a "safe place" to go to when I had anxiety or panic so I could calm myself down. She also taught me how to straighten out my body when I was in emotional or physical pain. My reaction to pain had been to stop breathing and curl up into the fetal position until the pain went away. Now, I was breathing and stretched out, which had the wonderful consequence of shortening the duration of the cycle vomiting attacks. Dr. Ann helped me through this very difficult time, fitting me into her busy schedule, and giving up her own lunch many times. When I got a little stronger, she suggested I find a therapist who could work more closely with me regarding the SRA.

I had already given up on finding a Christian counselor with SRA experience, so I prayed for guidance and chose blindly. I ended up with one counselor who leaned over the desk and with a voice used when one talks down to children said, "Does the government know?" I left in a hurry.

I did not give up on asking God for direction, so I asked again and chose blindly. This time God led me to a beautiful Christian woman who not only believed that SRA existed, but had counseled others with it before me. She was in a non-Christian behavioral health group, and I learned that most of the counselors at the clinic know of, believe, and help survivors of SRA. What a shock after all this time! Survivors were finally getting the specific help we so desperately needed.

I felt comfortable with Dr. Beverly right away. It was amazing how quickly she learned about my journey. Getting an outline of my life is quite an undertaking, but somehow, she kept it all straight. She quickly found out that I was a writer and would assign me topics to write about. One day, we talked about panic attacks. The attack has you overwhelmed by the emotions of the abused child inside you, yet with the mental capacity of an adult. She told me that the emotions were being expressed by the little girl inside and that she was still scared. She asked me to go home and write about her. My heart started pouring out through the words, and as I wrote I felt that hollow spot inside my chest start to ease in pressure. She helped me to set goals in life and enjoy the process. We are still working on helping my little one inside get healing, with the idea that I will then be able to control the emotions and not have them spin out of control. I have hope for the first time in what feels like forever.

Psalm 37:30

*The mouth of the righteous speaks
wisdom,
and his tongue talks of judgment.
(KJV)*

Song

"Breathe"
Jonny Diaz (Diaz, Smith, & Wood, 2015)

A Note from Dr. Beverly

~*~

Lisa walked through my door on a cold day in November. I saw anguish in her eyes as she told me about her journey from Satanic Ritual Abuse. My compassion reached out to her from my experience with counseling other SRA survivors. I knew what she was facing and I was determined to do what I could to help her find peace to move forward.

Over many months, I found out that Lisa had recently finished writing the first draft of Only God Rescued Me. The process of writing this memoir had taken a toll on her emotionally. She shared that she was battling horrible suicidal thoughts. I realized that she was also trying to cope with severe panic attacks that were robbing her of her ability to stay in the present and enjoy all the wonderful parts of life.

I was eager to get Lisa the help she needed, so we got right to work. We created coping strategies to get through the panic. Cognitive errors are a major part of the mental battles survivors face, and they were a big part of Lisa's current condition. It was a long process to look at one cognitive error at a time and to help her find a way to look at them differently so that she could move past them into a more positive thought life. We worked on the healing of her inner child, which was challenging for her. There were many times Lisa could not figure out how to reach that inner child nor know what to do when she did. We found that writing could bridge that gap for her. I encouraged Lisa to write to her inner child, and this provided Lisa a much needed outlet for her emotions.

It is also common for survivors of SRA to have Dissociative Identity Disorder. While dissociating helped Lisa to survive as a child, it was ineffective as an adult and was causing her to lose time. Lisa wanted to get rid of the dissociative walls and integrate each part that was originally created for survival. This integration made Lisa feel stronger and much more capable to cope with life's difficulties.

I shake my head in wonder at how far Lisa has progressed in such a short amount of time. She reports living most days, now, where she is happy and functional. Only God could have brought her so far and so quickly. Not only did God rescue her many years ago when she was first freed from the abuse, but He continues to rescue her today from all of the fallout the abuse left in her life. I rejoice with Lisa and agree wholeheartedly when she says, "Only God Rescued Me."

Dr. Beverly
DMin, MS, BC, LMHC, LCAC

Glimmer

Hope, as the thinnest of rays, tickles the horizon
I gaze at it and marvel
I have looked for it endlessly, but it was not there
The horizon was dark, almost always threatening,
But now I perceive it, a beautiful pink, tinged with rose
Smiling down at me

As I lift my head for the first time, I drink in the light
My soul yearns for more, I want all it has to offer
Rays of sunshine warm my frozen body
As the pain melts away
I want to dance in the warmth as I will be free
Then, I will spread my wings and soar

~*~

Epilogue

~*~

I am in my bathroom in the present. I have been vomiting in waves for hours. In between these episodes, I am rolling on the bathroom floor in severe abdominal pain and overwhelming nausea. My hair is in a ponytail to keep it out of the toilet, even though anything in my hair is painful for a migraine. The vomiting has put the migraine at a 10+ on the pain scale. James comes in with a pillow to cushion my head as I roll on the floor, and helps clean up the mess. He prays and does everything he can, but he is helpless to stop the agony.

I have been diagnosed with Cyclical Vomiting Syndrome. CVS is sheer torture. CVS, as well as many other conditions, is unfortunately common for a survivor of SRA. The body is damaged by the abuse, making it very difficult to get any kind of relief.

The whole concept of where to end this narrative of my life has been difficult for me to determine. I want you to have a concept of what "victory" for a survivor is. The problem is that I don't know what victory would look like. I wish I could tell you that I am perfectly healthy physically and emotionally, but that would not be true. The only way to view this healing process is to compare where I started my journey to where I am today. Still ahead lies the finish line, and although I get a glimpse of it, it still seems out of reach.

At the start of this journey, I spent many years in "survival mode." Every day was a challenge to live through. The emotional toll of getting the common, daily tasks completed was more draining that it should have been. When I started counseling, each session would leave me drained and triggered for a day or two.

My first priority was the physical and emotional needs of my family. My second priority was homeschooling. Homeschooling four children was difficult, and when 3:00 in the afternoon rolled around, I was tired. Then it was time for housework and dinner. Many were the nights I just couldn't pull dinner off, which is a pricey fallout that survivors have to pay. James, being the amazing man he is, was very understanding about this.

At any time and any place, I could have a flashback which could leave me numb for hours. There were months upon months of daily crying on the couch. Friendships were hard because there was no way to explain to people what I was going through. I wrote this during that time:

I weep and cry, and cry and weep
And when I'm done, I try to sleep
Then will come, another day
Where I can weep it too away

Because of the thousands of dollars spent on counseling, doctors, food and numerous other expenses that we would not have had if I had not been abused, money was always tight. The pressure of paying bills and knowing I was the cause for a lot of it, was hard to handle.

Officially, the criminal case against Father is still open. I have pondered this for many years but always come back to this point: I was obedient to what God was leading me to do. I do not understand God's reasoning or see the finished canvas, but whatever it is that He is doing is fine with me. I have found over time that the open criminal case has given me a cushion of safety. I know that it provides some level of protection, because in all these years, there has been no contact from my parents. I am thankful for this.

It is the responsibility of the parents to protect their children. Keeping their children safe from cults and away from the influence of people in the cults is a growing problem.

I still worry about the safety of my brothers' children. I take comfort only in the fact that I did all I knew to do to protect them from abuse. Sadly, my brothers did not listen to my warning. Knowing that my nieces and nephews might be current victims in a cult breaks my heart. A nightmare for me is one of my nieces or nephews coming to meet me later in life and wanting to know why I did not stop the abuse for them.

There is also the fallout of the "secondary trauma" that was inflicted on James and the kids because of my abuse and recovery. James always wanted to know what happened so he could help me through each flashback and memory, but it was very hard on him. What a courageous man!

As readers, you have journeyed with me now for many pages, and you have read some of what I have gone through. I have tried to be mindful of the trauma of reading what happened to me, so I have made the rituals and sexual abuse as general as possible, yet being enough to show how horrific SRA is.

So now I zoom out and look back at where I am today. I see God in every day of my life. Even when I felt I could not drag myself one more step, He encouraged and strengthened me in so many ways: hugs from my kids, the love of my husband, raising my children, enjoying the process of homeschooling, amazing pastors along the way that prayed for ,supported, and tried to understand me, a call from a friend at a particularly difficult time, Christian songs that would cycle in my brain, Bible verses that jumped into my mind that dealt directly with something I was struggling with, friends who tried hard to understand me in the midst of the physical and emotional trials, amazing counselors and psychiatrists, the beauty of the earth, the wonder at God's creation, and the list goes on and on… These were the gifts that God sent me at my lowest points. It was in each of these moments that His presence became so real, and these small gifts kept me focused on life. When I was at my worst, God was at His best.

I can clearly see that God has built a team around me to help. I have an amazing pastor. I felt the need to tell him of the SRA to make sure the satanic element of the abuse didn't bother him. I didn't want to be involved in any ministry if he felt uncomfortable about it. His response amazed me in that he smiled and said he could tell that I had received much healing and that my journey was not a problem for him. Here was another courageous man that God has placed in my life.

James really is an incredible man. He has been at my side this entire journey. He has been there through the pain and through the healing; never faltering in his faith that God would bring us through this together. He has done everything possible to keep me safe and help me through each day. I can't imagine what it would be like to be married to an SRA survivor, but somehow, he has done it. The promise we made to never divorce, he kept. He never abandoned me emotionally. The love that we have has certainly been tested over time, yet the closeness we now share has strengthened with the triumph over evil that we have endured. There are many days that I contemplate that outside of salvation, James is the most wonderful gift God has given me. I always know how much God loves me because of my James.

My children are older now and one by one they are tripping into their twenties. They have rallied around me through the years, knowing that there was something wrong with their mom, and jumping in to help in any way they could. Many were the pictures drawn and given to me to try to help my day be better. They learned what my triggers were and to this day still try to shield me from them. They have explained to their best friends who spent the most time in our house what was going on with me so that they wouldn't trigger me, and they would understand if I had a panic attack.

Once, when I was having a panic attack, my daughter Stephanie laid down next to me and quietly recited Psalm 23 in my ear. When I was sick, my children took over the house cleaning, cooking, and grocery store trips. When I had doctor appointments and could not drive myself because of pounding migraines, they would cancel what they had planned to take me to my appointment instead. They even took me to emergency rooms when James was at work.

My kids are strong and competent because of all they have learned in helping me. What an amazing gift they each have been! They are a safe place for me to run to. What a treasure I have been given.

My therapists have been there for me. Just thinking about the images that they have in their heads from my abuse makes me feel sad for them. Yet they have hung in there, and counseled me through many rough parts of my life. God used each one in a different area of recovery that I needed at the time. These Christian counselors are on the front lines of helping SRA survivors, and I cannot tell you enough about the courage and strength they exhibit without wavering. Never once did I have a counselor tell me that it was getting to be too much and they needed a few months break. Counselors are courageous to enter our lives, courageous to hear our experiences, and courageous to help us one day at a time.

Sadly, I have had numerous doctors in my recovery. For the first fifteen years, I did not say anything about abuse. Then, I slowly started realizing that my medical issues could stem from the abuse, and maybe this knowledge would help them to help me. For the last few years I have decided to tell the doctors that I am an SRA survivor upon the first visit. If they don't respond well, I know I need a new doctor. If they do respond well, they have background knowledge that helps them to know how to help me.

The first doctor I told was a neurologist, who had battled with me through a stroke and migraines for over ten years. She was amazing, always trying to help, and even took my very thick file home on weekends to see if there was something we hadn't yet tried. One day, I took a deep breath and told her about the SRA. Her eyes got huge as she looked at me and said, "Lisa, I have been working with you for years! Why haven't you told me this before?"

The reality was that I was scared. I didn't want to be doubted and was terrified I would be looked at like I was a crazy person. Her response as well as many doctors since, was one of empathy and gentleness.

I have had many pastors over the years as we have moved in our journey of life. I am so thankful for each one. They were there for us when we needed them and gave me space when it was necessary, even if it took a couple years. They sowed into James and the kids as well, helping them draw closer to God through this drama.

I am especially thankful for God placing Pastor Molnar in my life when I was seven years old. I decided to give God all of my heart and life to Jesus at a puppet show in his church. Through the years, I was given a strong knowledge of God and the Bible. This foundation of faith was what I held onto through all those years of abuse. Pastor Molnar came back into my life when James and I were beginning our healing journey, and he was just as sweet, kind, and strong in the Lord as ever. He helped me through so many great difficulties.

It has occurred to me that not all of the readers of this book will have the love of God in their lives and may still shy away from Jesus. I was only seven when I first decided that I wanted to be with God and that I loved Jesus for helping me to get right with Him. That childlike simplicity is really all that it takes to get your life safely into God's hands. In Romans 10: 9, the Bible says that if we say with our mouth that Jesus is Lord, and believe in our heart that Jesus was raised from the dead, then we are saved. I did just that and decided firmly to follow God the rest of my life. I am still walking it out that clearly today.

God loved me through my team. I learned to cautiously trust people with my past. God also lavished me with love through the beautiful passages of the Bible I have been sharing with you throughout this book. Just this morning I read Romans 8:18, "For I reckon that the sufferings of this present time are not worthy to be compared with the glory which shall be revealed in us."

SRA certainly produces a great amount of suffering because that is where the enemy has complete control. The Bible says that no matter what we suffer here on earth, it is nothing to be compared to how wonderful heaven will be. Therefore, I try not to focus on the horror I have seen down here, but keep looking forward to how amazing life will be in heaven.

I thank God for taking care of me in the abuse. I do not believe it was His plan for my life, but a result of others' sin. God is the Father I never had. Jesus is the brother I never had. In them I am well-loved and looked after.

So where am I now? The whole goal of SRA is to keep the child from ever being able to trust in God and to never tell anyone what happened to them. I broke both of those curses. I love God and trust Him with my life. Even though I went through horrible things, I was able to understand that He loved me and kept me; He rescued me and I did not self-destruct.

I have been able to explain SRA to people so that they can understand me better and one day I believe that I will help to educate people so they will learn how to minister words of healing to the victims and survivors.

It is only in His strength that I am able to walk free, and I do not take credit in my own strength unless I recognize His. I can look at my life from afar now and see the journey, the pitfalls, the mountains and valleys, and I recognize His hand leading me one step at a time. It took courage to believe that my body remembered the pain, and had its way of revealing my past to me. When my mind finally surrendered the memories, although I was flooded with fear, faith found its way to the surface, and in the valley He restored my soul.

I am now living my life, instead of existing in "survival mode." I make choices every day. I have many things I enjoy doing. I love spending time with God in the Bible, prayer, worship, and church. I enjoy playing the piano just for myself, because I understand I can do things merely because I enjoy them. My family is my passion in life, and I enjoy every moment I have with them. Going on walks with my James is always fun, as well as our little getaways. Writing is another love, and not only did I write this book, but I also blog. These are not little things to an SRA survivor, but huge. I am not living curled up and crying on the couch any longer. I am enjoying the world God gave me.

This doesn't mean the last year of my life wasn't difficult. It was. But between the hard days, are the days I am healthy and happy. The hard days get fewer and fewer; my body is getting healthier and I am at peace.

I would like to encourage SRA survivors who read this book. Healing is not easy and looks different for everyone. The biggest healing will come from God, as He is the Father that you never had. He protects you, loves you, and heals you. Jesus is the brother you never had, one who loves you and fills your heart with His love. Don't let the cult steal God or Jesus from you. Don't let them win. You are strong and with God you can make it.

To those reading this book to learn about SRA, I thank you for your courage. I pray that you will be able to help survivors in as little or big a way that God leads you. We survivors are a very hurt people and need a lot of love. Sit and cry with us from time to time. Just that emotional connection is amazing to us.

To the pastors, I thank you for taking time to read my story. Survivors are probably on the outskirts of your congregations, fearful and many times triggered. If they get courageous enough to tell you that they are a survivor, give them much love and grace. We can push hurt survivors away in a church society where people want an altar call to fix everything. Be gentle and spoon them the Word if they cannot handle a Bible on their own, which is triggering to many survivors.

To the family and friends of survivors, be strong for your loved one. There is no way they can express what happened or how horrible it was. Give them space when they need it and gentleness always. You will have to be brave and strong. Be grounded in the Word and your relationship with God. They will get better over time and you will love the healed person they are becoming.

To the cult active, child abusers, I say may God rebuke you. What you have done has severely damaged your young child. God is a God of mercy and grace, and you will need a lot of it. Get out of the cult, stay out, and get right with God. Satan has tried to steal God from you as well, so don't let him win.

I spent my life fantasizing of someone rescuing me. While the FBI never came and stopped it, God actually did. The rescue was not physical until my marriage to James, but it was spiritual. God kept me alive and protected His relationship with me. As I look back, a physical rescue would have been great, but temporary at best. The spiritual protection of my relationship with my Lord Jesus Christ was eternal and that's what I needed the most.

That dinner with my parents seventeen years ago started me on a path I never would have chosen to walk, but I am very grateful that I did in order to protect my children. They know about SRA from my experience, not theirs. I praise God for how He has brought me through the process. It is indeed true, that "Only God Rescued Me."

Psalm 40:2

He brought me up also out of an horrible pit, out of the miry clay, and set my feet upon a rock, and established my goings. (KJV)

Song

I Can Only Imagine
Amy Grant (Miller, I Can Only Imagine, 2003)

Song

I Am Free
New Life Worship (Egan & Furler, 2009)

Thanks

To you give I thanks
For making it through
The tragic story
I laid out for you

I hope you saw
Straight through to the end
That God above
Was always my friend

I pray He is also
Always with you
As you wrestle in what
He'd have you do

For reading this journey
Has opened your eyes
To the plight of survivors
Living world–wide

Special care will we need
To see through the tears
Treat us quite gently
The abuse went for years

God has been faithful
To get us this far
So you must use patience
As you slowly see scars

For show them we won't
Unless you we trust
After all of this time
It may not be much

Sit with us and cry
Give tissues for tears
Quietly whisper
A Psalm in our ears

Deuteronomy 20: 4

For the LORD your God is He that goes with you, to fight for you against your enemies,
to save you. (KJV)

John 16:33

These things I have spoken unto you, that in Me you might have peace. In the world you shall have tribulation: but be of good cheer; I have overcome the world. (KJV)

Ephesians 6:10

Finally, my brethren, be strong in the Lord, and in the power of His might. KJV

There Is a Line

There is a line, I did not draw
Stark and bold
Toward it I crawl
There's terror here
It yanks me back
I will not make it
I will crack

There is a line, I cannot see
I am lost
In great misery
I really can't
Go this trek
I am hopeless
Suicidal wreck

There is a line, that I am told
You can get there
My hand just hold
But hopeless am I
For what I don't know
There is no strength
For me to go

There is a line, I do not know
Why it's there
Or what it shows
But I will work
Scratch and claw
Cry and weep

Give it my all

There is a line, where terror still shrieks
Sunshine and peace
Each side loudly speaks
I listen to both
I look into mind
I have decided
To leave past behind

There is a line, behind I see
As it passed
It surprised me
Its silence spoke gently
It came and it went
I ponder it
What it meant

There is a line that I went over
It was just a moment
One step closer
I watch as the line
Fades far away
As I live in the moment
day by day
~*~

Acknowledgements

O_{nly} God Rescued Me came to be published after countless hours of prayer, helping, encouraging, painting, editing, reading, crying, and holding by a team of amazing and godly people that God has placed at key points throughout my life and in the creation of this book. I find it difficult to express my thanks in a manner suiting what each person has done when I cannot even mention their names for the sake of protection. So please gloss over the names and be amazed at the talent and time that have been given in the journey of this book.

Without God, there would be no story, no rescue, and no Lisa. To the one person I can name, He is, ironically, nameless to me. I thank my Lord and King, most Almighty God. He alone is my life and my fortress, my true God in whom I place all of my trust.

If I could tell you in all the ways my precious husband James has been there for me for the past twenty-six years, you would be as amazed as I am. He held me as I cried, only to go off and cry himself later. He gave me safety as he himself wrestled with how to do so. He ran interference when I was emotionally incapable of functioning. Every ritual was listened to because he wanted to know what I was dealing with so that he could help me. I am quite at a loss for how well he was prepared to be my husband. James and God worked hand in hand helping me through. A huge thank you to my James.

God blessed me with four amazing children. I would never have chosen the path for them that included the status as children of an SRA survivor, but they each walked it with compassion, help, strength, and love.

Stephanie has amazed me every day with her elegance and strength. She has shouldered much as she saw me at my worst and tried to watch after her younger brother and sisters. She has been a gift of joy to me since the day I first learned of her existence. From rubbing her through my tummy to hugging her today as a very talented and capable young woman, I see God's hand in her life, growing her through the difficulties. May God bless Stephanie richly for all she has done that no one has seen. Thank you, dearest Stephanie.

Daniel came into life early as my little knight in shining armor. Protecting me from a threat he didn't see or understand was very confusing when he was young. Protecting me from those he couldn't confront as a teen was very frustrating. Now he is a young man with the understanding of how dangerous yet fragile life is and how strongly he needs to look out for the welfare of those around him. His friends and family are very blessed. Thank you, sweet Daniel.

My powerful Anna has been my little Energizer bunny through the years. While my body tried so hard to kick her out in pregnancy, she determinedly hung on and has been strong ever since. She has been one who always wanted to know exactly what we were dealing with when I wasn't doing well. She has given me strength when I was weak and encouraged me when I felt I couldn't go on. She taught me to fight instead of fail. She taught me what family really means. Thank you, my faithful Anna.

Cleo is such a beautiful mix of her talented and deep thinking dad and her writing mom. Even as a toddler, she seemed to know much more about God that I could. She drew prophetic and encouraging power-pictures of being held in God's hand, beautiful rainbows, and every conceivable way for me to feel loved and cared for by God. Her somber eyes have carefully watched over situations through the years to make sure I wasn't being triggered or to make sure I was feeling safe. How one so young could understand so much is beyond my comprehension. God bless you, my darling Cleo.

For James' parents, Sue and Tim, I am speechless. They took me in as their own the minute I married their son, and when the flashbacks began, they were there for me in any way they could (and trust me, there were many!). My words are inadequate because they lovingly and capably supported James and me, and our children as well. Thank you to Sue above (I miss you every day), and to Tim who continues to bless us. You are the best.

Just the name of Pastor Molnar brings tears to my eyes. He brought me to God, taught me how to love God and the Bible, how to have faith, prayed with me to be filled with the Holy Spirit, and gave me the strength to keep going forward. He has been my life-long pastor, mentor, and counselor. If he hadn't shown up at a certain pharmacy, at a certain day, in a certain year, I may never have found God. Thank you, dear Pastor Molnar. Thank you.

Over the past seven years, my dear friend Denise was my first survivor friend. She talked to me, encouraged me, and just plain shared her life with me. She has brought to me so much understanding about the life of an SRA survivor. Thank you, Denise, I so enjoy being your friend!

My friend Nancy sat with me for hours and hours every week in college listening and sharing her life and mine. She gave me context and information that I needed to start to look at my family as something other than perfect. Thank you, Nancy.

Pastor Sluzas has so much faith, courage, and integrity. Thank you for walking with us through the valley and being the spiritual covering we needed in that dark time of our lives.

With Pastor T, our current pastor, I just shake my head. SRA never made him cower or pull back. He was full throttle in encouraging me to follow God in writing this book and giving my testimony. He has been a strong spiritual covering and continues to be incredible support. Thank you.

Pastor G, Pastor S, Pastor M, and Pastor K have each sowed into our lives what we needed for that point in our journey. They have all been wonderful and I thank God for their strong relationships with God and their ministry to me and my family. Thank you.

Oh, my many counselors. The soldiers on the front lines of my intersections with SRA. The nightmares must have been awful. Thank you, J, for all of the initial help of dealing with the fallout after that fateful dinner with my parents. Thank you J for teaching me what each feeling was (boy, did that take a long time-it sounded so easy). Thank you, E, for taking me on and ministering to me with EMDR and the theophastic, bringing so much healing in each ritual (I didn't think we would ever finish! Sorry for all the Kleenex I used!). To A, who got me through the suicidal battles while writing this book-you helped me to breathe. Thank you.

To my beloved teacher, M. Who knew that you would still be teaching me the same subject thirty-some years later? Some of us just never learn. Thank you for the prayers, the edits, and the friendship. You were there for me.

Thank you, Dolores. You were a friend to me when I was so low. You saw where I am now and you prayed me here.

I have had the blessing and privilege to meet so many SRA survivors in so many placed. They shared their lives and trusted me with their stories. Thank you! God bless you all!

Catherine was there at so many intersections of my life. I thank God for bringing her back into my journey when I needed direction and again bringing her back in when I was stuck with how to get this book published. God used her so many times in my life when we neither of us was even aware of it. Catherine, you are a blessing to many, and specifically a great blessing to me. Thank you!

Thank you to all the people I have not mentioned who have been there over the years. You are all wonderful and I am blessed.

Thank you, dear reader! May God bless you, keep you, and comfort you. Stay strong in Him.

Would you like to have Lisa speak at your church or event? You can find her at:

lisameister@onlygodrescuedme.com
onlygodrescuedme.com
"Only God Rescued Me" on Facebook

Scripture References

I Corinthians 15:57
Deuteronomy 20:4
Deuteronomy 28:11
Ecclesiastes 3:1-8
Ephesians 6:10
Isaiah 55:8-9
Isaiah 63:18-19
John 8:32
John 16:33
Joshua 1:9
Luke 8:17
Matthew 18:15-17
Proverbs 1:5a
Proverbs 3:5-6
Proverbs 5:21
Proverbs 12: 19 - 22
Proverbs 27:17
Psalm 6:6
Psalm 27:10-13
Psalm 37:1-7
Psalm 37:30
Psalm 40:2
Psalm 55:12-14
Psalm 91:4-5
Romans 8:18

Bibliography

Barrett, P., & Brown, A. (Composers). (2015). Good, Good Father. [C. Tomlin, Performer]

Brown, B. (Composer). (2006). Lord Reign in Me. [B. Brown, Performer]

Deviller, S., Hosier, S. S., & Lewis, M. (Composers). (1997). I Will Be Your Friend. [A. Grant, Performer]

Diaz, J., Smith, J., & Wood, T. (Composers). (2015). Breathe. [J. Diaz, Performer]

Cash, Edward; K. J. (Composer). (2009). Be Still. [K. Jobe, Performer]

Egan, J. C., & Furler, P. (Composers). (2009). I Am Free. [Worship, New Life, Performer]

Fielding, B., & Morgan, R. (Composers). (2006). Mighty to Save. [Hillsong, Performer] Sydney, Australia.

Gray, J. (Composer). (2014). Not Right Now. [J. Gray, Performer]

Green, S. (Performer). (2015). Household of Faith.

Hughes, T. (Composer). (2004). When the Tears Fall. [T. Hughes, Performer]

Lewis, C. (Composer). (1996). Beauty for Ashes. [C. Lewis, Performer]

Mandisa (Composer). (2013). Overcomer. [Mandisa, Performer]

Millard, B. (Composer). (2012). The Hurt & The Healer. [M. Me, Performer]

Miller, B. (Composer). (2003). I Can Only Imagine. [A. Grant, Performer]

Moen, D. (Composer). (2003). God Will Make a Way. [D. Moen, Performer]

Morgan, R. (Composer). (2002). Lord I Give You My Heart. [M. W. Smith, Performer]

Oksana, C. (2001). *Safe Passage to Healing: A Guide for Survivors of Ritual Abuse.* Lincoln: iUniverse.com.

Paris, T. (Composer). (1984). The Warrior is a Child. [T. Paris, Performer]

Chapman, Curtis; M. H. (Composer). (2003). Voice of Truth. [C. Crowns, Performer]

1 Corinthians 15:57

But thanks be to God, which giveth us the victory through our Lord Jesus Christ. (KJV)

Made in the USA
Coppell, TX
18 October 2022